Self-Parenting 12-Step Workbook

Windows To Your Inner Child

Patricia A. O'Gorman, Ph.D., and
Philip Oliver-Diaz, M.S.W.

Health Communications, Inc.
Deerfield Beach, Florida

Patricia A. O'Gorman, Ph.D.
Philip Oliver-Diaz, M.S.W.

© 1990 Patricia A. O'Gorman and Philip Oliver-Diaz

ISBN 1-55874-052-X

Publisher: Health Communications, Inc.
         3201 S.W. 15th Street
         Deerfield Beach, Florida 33442-8124

Cover design by Reta Thomas

ACKNOWLEDGMENTS

From Pat And Phil

To our fellow voyagers who have attended our self-parenting retreats and seminars and who so generously shared their experiences and allowed us to quote them here.

Also to Kate Dunham for being such a good sport, together with her loving support and dedication in editing our manuscript and to Elizabeth Grace for being there in the final proofing.

From Pat

To my brother Phil with whom I have shared and grown in this part of my journey, my gratitude for your vision and my love as you seek out new worlds.

To my husband Rob whose understanding, trust and tireless love gives me the courage to follow my heart.

From Phil

To Pat O'Gorman, my spiritual sister, who is my partner in the healing, friend to my inner child and inspiration; with sincere gratitude and love for all those dark nights when you held the candle.

To Sharon, my wife and best friend, who keeps teaching me the meaning of unconditional love and support and who keeps standing by me even when my path takes us far from home.

To Charlie who helped me open my heart to this book and taught me that love is all we need to know.

Dedication From Phil

. . . For all of us still struggling to be fully alive and still learning the lessons that love teaches us.

And From Pat

. . . To my sons, Jeremy and Michael, whose energy and wisdom teaches me again and again the meaning of being a child.

C O N T E N T S

To My Friends Interested In 12-Step Parenting Work

Dear Friend:

I would like to know if you are interested in learning more about 12-Step Self-Parenting, inner child or parenting materials. Drop me a note if you would like to attend a:

- Self-Parenting Retreat Or Seminar
- "Breaking The Cycle Of Co-dependency" Parenting Seminar Or Workshop

or if you are interested in more information on:

- "Self-Parenting" Inner Child Audio Tapes And Educational Materials
- "Breaking The Cycle Of Co-dependency" Parenting Audio And Video Tapes
- Material for educators and counselors.

I'm also interested in learning about groups who are using our steps and materials. Please write to:

Patricia A. O'Gorman, Ph.D.
568 Columbia Turnpike
East Greenbush, NY 12061

Older now, I know her . . .
And she survived . . .
The swift current of her blood runs in my veins.
From **The Great Miramichi Fire** by Joanne Dobson

Many of us are now finding the inner child who was hidden in the adult we grew up to be. In recovery, we are accepting our past and reconciling it to our present. In doing so, we are finding that recovery is possible as we learn to self-parent; to focus on ourselves, who we are, what we have been through, how we feel now and where we would like to go.

Inner child work is one process of recovery. Through it, we allow ourselves to travel the paths of our memories, to coax out of corners those associations we made in childhood that are so frightening we hide them, feelings so powerful that we have repressed them, memories so bittersweet we prefer not to experience them.

These guidebook exercises are presented as a means to an end not an end in themselves, for while inner child work is a powerful recovery tool, it is not recovery itself. It is always important to remember that in recovery the time needs to be right for each of us to begin the journey. It is important to plan and prepare for each stage along the way because sometimes, when the inner child has been invited in, feelings from the old traumas become too acute.

If you are an incest victim, have suffered repeated batterings as a child, have suffered a major trauma or are dealing with a profound issue in your life, you will need to let yourself know that, if you find yourself retraumatized as you invite your inner child in, then now is not the right time to begin inner child work.

If you are in therapy, you may want to consult your therapist about what you are learning through self-parenting. If you are not in therapy, be open to the idea that the support of a therapist and/or a recovery group may be helpful to you.

As you approach inner child work, be aware that its goal is not logical. You will not be marching through your unconscious, dealing with age three issues this week, age four issues next week and finally, at age 42, end up visualizing an inner child of exactly age 41. Inner child work is not notch-belt therapy where recovery is complete when you tick off all the issues imaginable. Rather, you are very likely to move back and forth across time, perhaps visualizing a child nursing peacefully at a mother's breast one time and a belligerent adolescent the next. Your memory banks are full. Let yourself embrace each memory you have and refuse to worry about those which have not yet come.

There is no need to be concerned with order in doing inner child work. You have not failed if you skip a year or if you remember something painful and decide not to continue working on this for months. The goal of inner child work is acceptance; acceptance of the child of the past, acceptance of your feelings about this child today.

In this inner child workbook, we offer you techniques we have developed and refined in our work with adult children of alcoholics and adult children of trauma. In the hope of validating your experience as you use the guidebook, we also offer you vignettes from the experiences of others who have used these techniques.

As you will realize, we have refined the concept of the inner child as we have developed the concept of self-parenting. Based on the 12 Steps of Alcoholics Anonymous, this inner child workbook and its companion, *12 Steps To Self-Parenting,* are about granting yourself a second chance to parent the child within. You may find your recovery work enhanced if you read both books. Together they represent an important tool in learning to nurture yourself through self-forgiveness and self-acceptance.

In our self-parenting retreats and seminars, we have been amazed and gratified by the ability each of us has to empower ourselves by freeing our inner child. In this spirit, we wish each of you a rewarding and wondrous adventure as you begin to embrace your own inner child.

With all our love,

Pat and Phil

INTRODUCTION

I used to be so happy
I used to be so gay
I used to play hide and seek
Run and skip and play.

Then you left me all alone
To try and ease the pain
Never knowing I'd hang around
Till we were friends again.

P.B., an ACoA

The Process

For many adult children of alcoholic and dysfunctional families, the recovery process can feel as if it uncovers more pain than can ever be resolved. The need to explore the past in order to come to terms with it initiates fear because the process is so filled with uncertainty that it seems to promise more hurt than fulfillment.

At the outset we are confronted by the fact that we are strangers to ourselves. We do not know how we feel. We do not know what we think.

We cannot remember our past and we become increasingly uncertain of our future. We may find ourselves seeking completion through something or someone outside ourselves. Inside we secretly feel we are only half-persons, for we have not yet learned to look within and identify our strengths. We have not yet met our true selves.

Higher Parent And Inner Child

The true self is comprised of two vital cores: our inner child and our Higher Parent. Our inner child is the center of our love, our feelings, our spontaneity, our curiosity. It is that part of us which is exquisitely alive, vital, creative and from which we draw our energy. It is the part of us that feels our pain, anger and rage. Our inner child knows fear. She needs love, tenderness and support and feels hopeless without them.

Our Higher Parent is the gentle center of our inner wisdom and intuitive knowledge. Our Higher Parent knows what is best for our inner child, protects her and is her advocate in the outside world. Our Higher Parent is objective and problem-solving, the part of us that acts as a loving guide to our inner child. Our Higher Parent is also transcendent, being the aspect of ourselves that is a direct channel to our Higher Power.

Vulnerable Cores

These cores of our being are vulnerable. They can be traumatized by living through the abuses of a dysfunctional family. One result of this trauma is that the inner child is deprived of the wisdom of the Higher Parent. The inner child may then develop defenses that lead to a co-dependent, or compulsively dependent, orientation to the world.

Co-dependency is a result of our having learned and internalized other viewpoints or voices that mask the nature of our true being. The true self speaks with two voices, that of our inner child and that of our Higher Parent. We incorporate other voices as an attempt to deal with the traumas we experience during childhood. Co-dependency means that the inner child, alone and without the Higher Parent, is directed by these other voices, such as the voice of a critical adult who accuses the child of wrongdoing which requires punishment. It is only through the struggle to deal with co-dependency that we can learn how to silence the voices that devalue us and free our true selves to speak again.

This workbook invites you to become familiar once more with your true self. You are invited to learn how to re-establish a dialogue between the inner child and Higher Parent within yourself. You will be guided in this process through visualizations that allow you to interact with your inner child and your Higher Parent, exercises that allow you access to these two voices and experiences designed to bring your true self to light.

Co-dependency

In co-dependency we learn to present false faces to the world. The inner child is locked away for fear her spontaneity will cause embarrassment, humiliation or overwhelming pain. The voice of the Higher Parent is silenced for fear it will rock the family's already unsteady boat by offering an alternative point of view or by questioning a sacred belief. The honest responses of both inner child and Higher Parent are extinguished for fear they may cause rejection or worse — abandonment.

The co-dependent child has learned to be helpless. In her fear, she ceases questioning what is around her and begins to invalidate her own perceptions. She feels there is little she can do to make life better except turn off the pain she feels and try to reduce the pain of those around her. However, because she is only a child, she has few skills available to help her family and she fears challenging them beyond what she believes they can tolerate. In her helplessness, she pulls inside herself and stops growing. This lack of emotional growth results in her remaining fixed in her childhood beliefs about the world and about her family until her recovery begins.

. . . A Decision To Survive

What is co-dependency but a decision to survive? Rather than face the possible disintegration of her support system, the child makes a shrewd choice: to survive. Rather than take care of her own needs, rather than validate her own reality, the child begins taking care of the needs of those on whom she depends for survival. But in this largely unconscious game of bartering self for survival, neither child nor family wins.

The Co-dependent Self: Its Legacies

Unresolved Childhood Traumas

A family tradition of co-dependency does not permit the resolution of childhood traumas. As a result the inner child is frozen in a state of silent grieving, incapacitated by the hard pain of childhood.

. . . Hard Pain — The Pain Of Resistance

Hard pain is the pain of resistance. Hard pain is the pain of childhood. It is the pain that says, "They did this to me and they should be punished. They are evil." Hard pain is the pain of resentment and hate. Hard pain is the pain that will not end as long as all of our energy is spent in justifying how wronged we have been and how sorry for ourselves we must feel. Hard pain keeps us stuck in the past.

Dark-Side Defenses

Dark-side defenses are those developed during the darkness of childhood trauma. They are defenses generated by the traumatized child in an effort to make sense of her world. They are defenses that protected the inner child when they were created. They provided safety in a world that did not feel safe — and for this the inner child will be forever grateful.

Dark-side defenses did their job in protecting the inner child. These same defenses continue to function but at an increasingly high cost as years pass. Not only are they worn out through overuse but they are maintained with such loyalty that they tend to suppress the development of more flexible defenses that will enhance the inner child.

As a result of this lack of development, the adult child's defenses are based only on the knowledge the young inner child had available when the defense was put in place. Because she is still deprived of the guidance of her Higher Parent, she finds the world as frightening as she did when she was a child.

Unfulfilling Relationships

The co-dependent self that emerges from this family system is often controlling, needing to rescue others or to be rescued by them. The co-dependent self may turn to other things in her search for completeness. Compulsive overeating, compulsive sex, compulsive spending or excessive time spent working are all fruitless attempts to become filled up, to become whole.

The co-dependent self has learned to exist as a half-person, only complete when something or someone external can be drawn inside. She has lost access to her inner child. As a result she has lost her capacity for playfulness, intimacy and true sexuality. She has lost access to her Higher Parent and, deprived of inner guidance, she repeats these unsuccessful patterns in each new relationship she tries to form.

An Extraordinary Need For Control

The need for control is not unique to children of alcoholics. From the beginning of time, legends and myths have spoken of this need as being part of the human condition. What is often different about children of alcoholics is our extraordinary need to control, not for the sake of specific outcomes but to avoid vulnerability to any outcome we cannot direct. It is not surprising that our feelings are the first part of us to bear the brunt of this need to control.

. . . Resulting In Becoming Compulsively Self-Reliant

As children of alcoholics, we are often taught the family tradition that to survive we must be self-sufficient at all costs. We are instructed to trust only in our will to make things happen. Our trust in our will and our belief that we are alone in the world leave us secretly following the family tradition of bitterness and hopelessness, although the world rarely realizes what is happening.

For our inner child, self-will and total self-reliance are the only known protections. This self-sufficiency becomes part of our store of compulsive behavior and often leads to us having difficulty, even inability, in forming intimate relationships. We become unable to receive from our loved ones, who eventually resent us for acting superior but, simultaneously, demanding that they "be there for us."

Finally, many of us conclude we cannot trust our feelings. We decide we can trust only our intellect and attempt to rely on reason alone. For some, even falling in love becomes an intellectual exercise, determined by counting shared characteristics, not by feelings of attraction. Our addiction to self-reliance may even separate us from our faith in God. We become completely isolated, prisoners in cages of our own construction, rulers over tiny kingdoms only we inhabit.

Fear Of Abandonment By God And By Others

For all of us fear is the darkroom in which negatives are developed. When our defensive belief in our ability to control replaces childhood faith in a Higher Power, it is an easy step to transfer the emotional abandonment felt at home to a sense of abandonment by God for leaving us in a place so bereft of hope. Our anger at God then leaves us floundering in despair, searching for some meaning in our lives beyond sheer survival.

... Becoming Addicted To Empty Wells

Many of us learn to survive with minimal expectations from life. We learn to expect little, not only from parents but also from co-workers, spouses and partners. Our limited expectations become self-fulfilling prophecies as we unconsciously begin to search out relationships with those who appear safe and familiar, "empty wells" who will not fulfill our needs. In this way many of us maintain our ties to our childhoods, choosing people to marry, to live with or to love, who have the same limitations we knew in our family members.

The Promises Of Inner Child Work Through Self-Parenting

Inner child work is about freeing our inner child and releasing the voice of our Higher Parent. Inner child work is about accepting and nurturing the self. The promise of inner child work is that we will be able to live in the present and leave the past behind.

Making Hard Pain Soft — Resolving Childhood Traumas

Soft pain is the pain of healing. It is a pain of sometimes agonizing depth but it carries the promise that "This too shall pass." Soft pain may demand that the villain receive justice but it listens to the reassurance of the Higher Parent that there are few true villains and many loyal soldiers. Soft pain leads us to greater understanding and wisdom as we grow in compassion. Soft pain leads eventually to peace.

We can welcome soft pain, for in its darkest depths, healing is underway. We can feel ourselves opening to reconciliation and the knots in our stomachs loosening. The birth of serenity has begun.

Self-Acceptance, Self-Forgiveness

Self-acceptance results from living in the present. Self-acceptance is the gift we give ourselves when we look openly at our inner child and our Higher Parent and bear witness to their existence within us. From this we learn to value all that we are and all we can become.

Allowing A Spiritual Awakening

Allowing a spiritual awakening is all about letting God into our lives and learning how to reach out for love. It is about letting go of the baggage of the past, healing old wounds and learning how to avoid recreating these painful patterns in our present. It is about allowing our inner child to be spontaneous, joyful, alive, free. It is about allowing our Higher Parent to guide us with inner wisdom.

Creating Intimacy

A spiritual awakening is about learning to join our Higher Parent and inner child together in a healthy manner, making possible true intimacy with others and breaking the isolating bonds of compulsive or co-dependent behavior. It is about learning through self-parenting to join with our Higher Parent and follow him trustingly through the dark times while our inner child makes her healing energy of love available to us and those around us.

... All On The Road To Recovery

All of this constitutes the process of recovery. Self-parenting is about the long road home, the road from loneliness and self-doubt to intimacy and self-validation. As we travel the road home, we move from the pain of the past to the joy and fullness of the present.

Ways To Use The Guidebook

Rediscovering Your Inner Child And Your Higher Parent

Our guidebook is designed to reacquaint you with the two voices of your true self, that of your inner child and of your Higher Parent. These two voices will be used exclusively throughout the guidebook. It is only through restoring and maintaining the dialogue between these two vital cores that you can free yourself to be the complete individual you were born to be.

Beginning A Process

What we hope to begin in this guidebook is a process, not an inscription in stone. You can use the material creatively, in any of a number of ways, from a one-time marking of where you are in recovery to regular reworking of the self-parenting steps.

Alone Or In A Group

There are at least five ways the guidebook can be used:

1. Follow what is proposed, working on your own.
2. Skip around, focusing initially on those steps which have the most meaning for you now, leaving the others for later.
3. Do the same exercises at different points in your recovery to mark your progress.
4. In a group, have the leader guide you in the visualizations and written exercises, then share your responses with others.
5. Work on your own at home, then bring in the exercises to share with other participants in your group.

Remember, there is no *right* way to learn more about your inner child and your Higher Parent. There are many different paths, all varying in length, yet all leading to the same final destination. Taking the first steps on the journey to your true self is what is important, wherever you start.

Enjoy the process of learning who you truly are.

CHAPTER 1

Surrendering
And Control

Self-Parenting Step 1:

Admitted our powerlessness to change our past — that our lives had become unmanageable and became willing to surrender to our love and not to our fear.

To be is to love.

The words of Prahsingh in **Brother Lion** *by Jeanne Livingston*

I have been alone and unprotected for too long. I want us to be close now — an important part of each other's lives. I want you to love me, cherish me and protect me, like you do your kids. I love you so very much. Do you love me?

Excerpt from N.J.'s letter from her inner child

Surrendering To Our Love For Our Inner Child

How many times have we asked ourselves the question — "Do I love myself?" So often we take ourselves for granted, assuming a burden that we would never accept from anyone else. Sometimes we even treat ourselves as if we do not like, let alone love, ourselves. To change this pattern we need to learn to surrender to our love for our inner child.

Surrendering to this love does not have to be a complicated process. It is actually quite simple. All that is required is that we open ourselves to our inner child. We allow ourselves to begin to experience life two-dimensionally, on both an emotional, or inner child, and a cognitive, or Higher Parent, level. We do this consciously at first, knowing that soon this act of checking in at once with our inner child and our Higher Parent will become spontaneous.

As we practice this change, we know that we may feel unexpected, sometimes even unwanted, emotions. We may begin to feel angry, afraid, overwhelmed and abandoned. We may also begin to feel such intense joy and peace that we become dizzy on top of the emotional heights.

Surrendering to our love for our inner child means allowing ourselves to feel all of our feelings, knowing that attempting to deny any of them only wastes energy. This is energy we can better invest in solving or enjoying our feelings.

Surrendering to our love for our inner child also means loving ourselves through the realization and the expression of all our feelings. This means loving ourselves even when we feel angry or frightened or in a rage. Our self-love is based on acceptance, not self-judgment. To love ourselves is to accept ourselves, without self-accusations or pretenses.

To know and to love ourselves, we need to carve out peaceful moments in our lives. "A quiet mind cureth all," said Robert Burton and so, in our guidebook exercises, we will seek to re-establish the quiet that was naturally within us when we were children.

Learning About — You

Let us begin to invite in our inner child.

Prepare by focusing your eyes on a point in front of you and breathing deeply.

Allow your thoughts to drift to your inner child. Ask her guidance as you start writing the story of your life.

Let yourself listen; write down what you hear.

Now read over what you've written. What strikes you most about your life's story?

What type of life have you had?

How do you feel about your life so far?

Loving Ourselves In Our Lives

Loving ourselves is our birthright. This is how we entered the world. This is how we initially related to the world. Loving ourselves is not a process apart from our lives but is what our life is about. To love ourselves is to be ourselves, to experience ourselves. This means allowing our spontaneity, our curiosity, our feelings to be revealed. To be, to live is to love.

Let us begin the process of surrendering to our love for our inner child by inviting her to return. Focus your eyes on a point just ahead and breathe deeply.

Allow your thoughts to drift to your inner child.

Allow yourself to look upon the face of your inner child. Allow yourself to reach out and touch her, to stroke her cheek, caress her hair. Allow yourself to hold her, to love her.

Allow yourself to see yourself and your inner child. Write down what you see.

Remember that our inner child has no one face, no fixed age. Initially she may come to us as an image remembered from a photograph or simply as a feeling, without a physical presence. At times she may not even be physically familiar. At other times, our visualizations will rapidly change, like fast-paced snapshots each showing a different feeling state.

Some of us will find we cannot easily picture an inner child. We should not be disturbed. In time, through patient inner child work, she will feel safer and appear more fully. The most important part of our imaging is to follow our feelings, to "go" with our inner child however she appears to us.

Allow the image that came to you. Accept it, for it is a part of you.

Write a brief letter to your inner child, telling her how you feel about her.

Read over the letter. What do you feel is the most important statement that you made to your inner child?

Prepare now to ask your inner child to speak to you.

Focus your eyes on a point just in front of you. Breathe deeply. Ask her to write a brief letter to you, stating how she feels about you.

Read her letter. What do you feel is the most important point your inner child is trying to make to you?

Prepare now to have a dialogue with your inner child.

Focus on an object in front of you, breathe deeply and ask your inner child, "How do you know you are loved?"

Allow your focus to return and then write down what she has said.

Again, focusing on a nearby object, breathe deeply and ask your inner child, "How do you know I love you?"

Allow your focus to return and then write down what she says.

Again, focus your eyes just ahead of you, breathe deeply and ask your inner child, "When you are angry or afraid, do you feel my love for you?"

Allow your focus to return and then write down your inner child's response.

Settle your focus on a nearby object. Breathe deeply and allow yourself to feel how it would be to love your inner child unconditionally, even when she is angry and afraid.

Write down your feelings.

Return your focus to an object near you and continue to breathe deeply. Ask your inner child, "How best can I show my love for you?"

Write down what she says.

Now prepare to speak with your Higher Parent, that part of each of us that is wise and knows the answers. Breathe deeply and focus on a point just in front of you.

Ask your Higher Parent, "What blocks do I place in the way of loving myself?"

Write down what you hear.

Now ask your Higher Parent, "What obstacles do I place in the way to stop others loving me?"

Write down what your Higher Parent says.

Compare the two lists. Are there some blocks which are the same?

List these:

From this list, choose one block and focus on it.

Ask your Higher Parent what you can do to begin to remove this block.

Listen, and write down what your Higher Parent says.

Understanding Why We Feel We Need To Control

Once we surrender ourselves to loving our inner child, we can begin to address our past pattern of filling ourselves with the illusion of control instead of the reality of love.

It has been said that control is the one drug of choice for adult children of alcoholics. The need to control did not spring up in one day. It developed over time as a result of the lack of validation we received from those around us. We saw and we experienced but our observations were not confirmed. In fact, they may have been contradicted. Some of us heard our parents arguing and threatening to get a divorce only to be told, "Nothing is wrong." Some of us saw a mother's black eye or heard our parents threaten to kill each other, only to be told we were imagining things. Our families in times of stress sounded much like the members of the court in the children's story *The Emperor's New Clothes*. The courtiers complimented the emperor's nonexistent clothes, rather than confront the fact he was naked. Like them, our parents were unable to validate us or our experiences at important times in our lives.

Others of us may have found our need for control developing from a frustrated drive for mastery. As children we enjoyed gaining competence — in walking, talking, running, reading with Mommy or playing ball with Dad. Our sense of mastery arose from our growing capacity to do, to influence, to see ourselves empowered in the world. Our mastery needed to be acknowledged, complimented and nurtured.

However, in families torn with strife, our achievements may have gone unnoticed. We may not have received the attention or recognition we needed. We may not have been taught how to bring balance into our lives, that, for example, it is good to rest after a hard push toward a goal. We may not have been shown how to measure our accomplishments nor how to give ourselves credit for a job well done.

Let us prepare to talk with our Higher Parent and our inner child about why we are "control junkies," feeling trapped by our superhuman attempts at mastery.

Focus on a nearby object and breathe deeply.

Ask your Higher Parent to help you list all the aspects of your life you are trying to control.

Write down what your Higher Parent says to you.

Circle the control issues that cause the most problems for you.

Choose one of the issues you have circled. Focus on a nearby object, breathe deeply and ask your Higher Parent how you can begin the process of letting go of control over this aspect of your life.

Write down what your Higher Parent says to you.

Let us now turn to our inner child and try to gain access to her voice in a different way. We will use a simple technique which strikes at the heart of control: writing with the "opposite hand."

Those of us who are right-handed will write with our left hands; those of us who are left-handed will write with our right hands. (It may be easier to write this way with a pencil rather than a pen.)

Pick up your pen or pencil. Breathe deeply.

Ask your inner child, "What do you fear will happen if you stop trying to control?"

Write down her answer.

The Price Our Inner Child Pays For Our Need To Control

We each pay a price for our actions. Often this price is unconscious and we can check what it is simply by making our feelings conscious. Sometimes this process can begin when we admit to ourselves that we do not know how we feel.

Then, as inner child work continues, we can actually get in touch with some core issues, such as fear of intimacy, fear of spontaneity, compulsive self-reliance, guilt, rage and fear of our own empowerment.

We may be surprised at the patterns we try to maintain, the measures we are willing to take just to avoid facing our own vulnerability. It is important, as we begin to address our control issues, that we do not try to tackle them all at once. Small steps here can yield great results — opportunities to love and nurture ourselves.

Let us prepare to speak again with our inner child.

Focus on a nearby object. Breathe deeply and ask your inner child, "What price do you pay for your need to control?"

Write down her answer, using your opposite hand.

Ask your inner child, "Do you want to continue paying this price?"

Write down what she says, using your opposite hand.

Now ask your inner child, "What help do you need to begin to give up control?"

Write down what she says, using your opposite hand.

Affirming What We Now Believe

Affirmations are a means of clarifying and reinforcing our new intentions to nurture ourselves. Affirming statements, such as, "I will be guided by my love and not by my need to control," give us clear and conscious guideposts on the road toward change.

Affirming what we believe and intend to do is part of our surrendering to our love for ourselves. By allowing us to repeat our new intentions again and again and again, affirmations are an important part of our healing.

Ask your inner child now to write some affirmations that support the work you have done on this step.

Remember As Children . . .

We loved ourselves totally.

We loved ourselves and others independently of what we or they were feeling.

We sought not to control but to master.

We knew only the goodness in ourselves and in others.

We were content to live in the present.

We looked within ourselves for answers.

We knew our true selves.

Guidelines

Establish a daily dialogue with your inner child. Invite your inner child into your lap at home; to play with your own children; to be with you at work, especially when you are under stress. Invite your inner child to be with you when you are with the very special people in your life.

Also seek your inner wisdom. Invite in the voice of your Higher Parent at those key moments in your life.

Practice loving yourself no matter what you are feeling.

Tell your inner child daily that you love her.

Allow yourself to experience your feelings while you practice letting go, in the safe presence of your Higher Parent.

Give yourself the gift of daily affirmations and meditations. Begin by reading those in the book *12 Steps To Self-Parenting* and then expand upon them by writing your own.

CHAPTER 2

You And Your Higher Parent

Self-Parenting Step 2:

Found hope in the belief that recovery is possible through faith and an acceptance of the fact that we are never really alone.

Growing means to open yourself to the breath of heaven and at the same time to sink roots into the darkness of the earth.

Joseph Gallagher

To My Higher Power

You don't give me much of what I want — but in my heart I know you do take care of me and know what I need to grow and be fulfilled.
I'm still angry at you for bringing me into an alcoholic home when I was born but I wouldn't be in a position to break the cycle and — most of all — to become whole if I didn't go through all the pain and hurt.
But I still ask, "Why me?" and "What's next?"
Stay tuned: I trust your wisdom. I know you love me — I can feel it and it feels so good.

Excerpt from J.C.'s letter to his Higher Power

Emotional Abandonment

The goal of inner child work is to resolve feelings from childhood, to make sense of those feelings and then to move on with our lives. Abandonment is one of the primary feelings many of us have experienced in childhood and still experience now. In one way or another as children from dysfunctional families we feel we were abandoned. Some of us never knew our biological parents and were brought up by adopted parents or in foster homes or institutions. We may have concluded that this was due to a failing in us, that we were the problem, that we were abandoned because we did something bad. We may have felt we would be rejected or abandoned again if we showed our true feelings.

Though most of us were brought up with our biological parents, we still felt abandoned because their problems interfered with their ability to care for us with any consistency. Again we may have concluded that it was our needs that were causing the problem.

In either case we felt abandoned emotionally as children. This feeling of abandonment has affected our relationship with our Higher Power. Many of us were left angry and bitter at God. The first step to spiritual recovery is to take the journey from anger and bitterness to faith and hope.

The Long Journey To Faith And Hope

This is a long journey for most of us. The first step is to face how we truly feel. In order to create a pathway from our heart to our Higher Power we will need to see the real face of our anger. At the core of the bitterness within us lie our feelings of abandonment. We avoid these feelings because our inner child fears that we will not be able to survive feeling them. Our inner child reacts to the abandonment as though it's still going on and he is still helpless to do anything about it.

Let us prepare to face our feelings of abandonment.

Invite your inner child into your consciousness.

Visualize your inner child coming toward you. See him and let him come close. Breathe deeply.

Let him tell you his feelings from childhood about being left to take care of himself.

It is important to validate our inner child's feelings and his reality. What felt real when we were children was real to us. All too often we minimize the reality of our childhood. We make excuses for our parents instead of saying, "This is how I felt" and we fail to give ourselves credit for overcoming so many difficult obstacles.

Write a letter to your inner child telling him how much respect you have for him.

Let him know you appreciate how hard it was for him to be his own parent as he grew up.

Focus your eyes on a point in front of you, breathe deeply and ask your inner child to tell you who and what he needed to take care of him when he was growing up.

Allow your focus to return.

Write down what your inner child said to you during the course of this visualization.

Children Of Loyalty

Although we all had different backgrounds there was one characteristic most of us had. We were loyal. We stood by our parents even when their self-centered behavior hurt us. We were dutiful. We took care of our parents and our siblings. We stood by them even when they would not stand by us in the way we needed. We were good loyal soldiers even at five or six years of age.

This sense of misguided, even compulsive, loyalty often contaminates our relationships in adult life. We stay hopelessly stuck in negative relationships or marriages where our chief job is to repair someone else while we are left empty and unfulfilled. We create a world full of people with nothing to give instead of finding people who can nurture us. As Thomas Merton said, "The biggest human temptation is . . . to settle for too little." This is exactly what happens to many of us children from dysfunctional families.

From Empty Wells . . .

Many of us have become addicted to being abandoned by others. We find ourselves in empty-well relationships with people who are incapable of meeting our emotional needs. This is a recreation of our childhood situation where we were abandoned, physically or emotionally, by our parents.

By choosing to marry, to live with and to love people who have the same limitations we experienced within our families we maintain our ties to our childhood.

In order to change this scenario we must first identify the nature of the relationships in our lives. It is necessary to name the empty-well relationships and to identify the takers and givers in our lives so we can make healthy, self-affirming decisions about who we let into our lives.

Let us prepare to review the relationships in our lives.

Breathe deeply and focus on an object in front of you.

Ask your Higher Parent, the source of inner wisdom and guidance, to help you list all the people you take care of in one way or another and how you take care of them.

Clear your thoughts and write down what your Higher Parent said.

. . . To Full Wells

This is the reality of our lives. These are the empty-well relationships in our lives. This is the ugly face of co-dependency in our lives. We have hidden our feelings about this reality. We have justified our existence by feeling the pain of others and have not felt the pain all this causes us. We must face our pain if we are to be free.

Focus your eyes on an object in front of you and breathe deeply.

Allow your thoughts to drift to your inner child. See him standing before you.

Let him tell you how he feels about your list of empty-well relationships.

When he has finished, write down what he said.

Ask your inner child how he feels about the way you've treated him while you were taking care of everyone else.

Let him tell you.

Now prepare to ask your Higher Parent for assistance.

Clear your thoughts of everyday concerns.

Ask your Higher Parent to help you find the real reason you sacrifice yourself and your inner child's happiness for people who use and abuse you.

Write the answer.

Is it worth it?

The way out of the continual pattern of empty-well relationships is to create full-well relationships, that is, to find people who can give as well as receive. We need help in learning how to raise our expectations of how others will treat us and how to reject people who continue to use us.

Ask your Higher Parent to help you to identify ways for you to bring full-well relationships into your life.

Focus your eyes on a nearby object. Let your consciousness drift.

Allow yourself to refocus and then write down what you have experienced.

When We Become God

One common reaction to our childhood abandonment is the replacement of a Higher Power in our lives by self-will and self-reliance. For most of us, learning to depend on ourselves was necessary for our survival. Unfortunately we continue to behave as though we are still in a world where we can depend on no one and nothing else but ourselves. We have become compulsively self-reliant, trapped in a cage of our own making.

Our self-reliance has also separated us from those we love and from our friends and co-workers. For example, we often find it necessary to do everything ourselves because we think we do things better. People close to us may want to leave us when they feel unneeded — as though they have no role in our lives.

Prepare to ask your Higher Parent for assistance.

Clear your mind of everyday things.

Ask your Higher Parent to help you make a list of times when your self-reliance has separated you from other people.

Examine the list. How much does your self-reliance separate you not only from people but from your Higher Power?

Abandonment By God

In order to move forward it is necessary to come face to face with our true feelings about our Higher Power. For some of us this is no problem because we have forged a positive relationship with our Higher Power over the years. But for others there is still a great deal of pain associated with our relationship to our Higher Power.

As we were growing up some of us had negative experiences with organized religion. Others of us may have felt abandoned by our Higher Power and denied its existence. We may have prayed that the family arguments and drinking would stop and when they didn't, we felt unloved, alone and forgotten by God. As a result we have lost the spiritual guidance available to us. In order for us to reclaim this guidance we must clear out the negative feelings to make room for a positive relationship with our Higher Power.

Prepare to invite in your inner child.

Focus on a point in front of you. Imagine yourself in a favorite place. Settle into this place.

Now imagine your inner child is there with you.

Let your inner child tell you his feelings about God.

Allow your focus to return. Now write a letter to your Higher Power describing the feelings you experienced.

The Way Back To God

Most of us have the same concept of God that we had as children. Our concept of the world around us changes and matures. Our concept of ourselves matures. However, many of us hold fast to a childish concept of God. Sadly, we often see him as a bad parent who has abandoned us in our time of need.

The way back to God starts with facing our concept of him, letting our inner child share his feelings about God. Then we can create a more mature concept of God, one that accounts not just for the pain but also for the love there is in the world.

We begin by opening ourselves to the experience of coming face to face with our Higher Power, as we understand Him. In this we are guided by the wisdom of our Higher Parent.

Prepare to meet your Higher Parent.

Allow your eyes to focus softly ahead of you and breathe deeply.

Visualize your Higher Parent coming toward you. Now visualize you and your Higher Parent walking together. Share your troubles and your fears with your Higher Parent.

Let your Higher Parent comfort and counsel you. Listen as your Higher Parent guides you.

Write down your experiences during your visualization.

Getting beyond the resentment we have toward our Higher Power allows us access to His wisdom and insight. Acknowledging our faith in a power greater than ourselves allows us to realize that we are never truly alone. Believing that recovery is possible through faith opens the door to limitless growth and self-actualization.

Remember that our feelings are only part of the story. They represent what our inner child harbors inside. It is essential to remember that our feelings do not constitute our entire being. We also have our Higher Parent to help us.

We have the resource of our Higher Parent's wider perspective on any problem or life issue we face. We do not need to be lost in confusion anymore. Our Higher Parent can supply all the guidance we need so we can reach the source of true security, our Higher Power as we understand Him. As long as we have faith in that Higher Power we are never really alone and we can change the course of our lives.

Remember As Children . . .

We felt an intimate personal connection to our God.

We felt a connection to the world around us and we rejoiced in this.

We spoke freely to God and asked for help when we felt help was needed.

We freely gave to those we loved.

We freely received what those we loved had to offer us.

We were able to feel our anger at God and our loved ones.

We were able to admit to our hurt feelings, feel the pain and move on with life.

Guidelines

Own your feelings of abandonment and the impact they have had on your faith in a Higher Power.

Allow yourself to face the empty-well relationships in your life.

Learn that you can create full-well relationships in your life.

Own your compulsive self-reliance and your reasons for it so that you may begin to set yourself free.

Recognize the inner wisdom available to you through your Higher Parent.

Realize that just as you reconcile other relationships, you can reconcile your relationship to God.

CHAPTER 3

Learning How To Reach Out For Help

Self-Parenting Step 3:

Learned to let go of compulsive self-reliance by reaching out to our Higher Parent.

Thank you Lord for all you have given me.
Thank you Lord for all you have taken
away from me.
And thank you Lord for all you have left me.

AA Prayer

Dear Higher Power,

Over the years I have had a hard time believing in
you, much less understanding you. Many times I have
felt so abandoned and all alone. I didn't believe in
anyone but me. That belief, though, has brought me
pain and made me feel abandoned. I have been so
isolated. I now need your help to trust . . . to reach
out to others . . .

Excerpt from N.H.'s letter to her Higher Power

Compulsive Self-Reliance

The thought of reaching out for help or letting go of self-reliance often raises a red flag for adult children from dysfunctional families. Compulsive self-reliance is the biggest issue most of us face. We have been taught to be self-sufficient at all costs and to trust only in our own will to make things happen. This self-sufficiency often inhibits our ability to *let go and let God.*

As children, we found it easy and natural to reach out and ask for help without shame or reservation. At some point in our childhood, however, we realized that we could not rely on help coming from our parents and we needed to take care of ourselves. This gave birth to our compulsive self-reliance.

As children we gave and expected unconditional love. What we often received from our parents was conditional love. Our parents gave us the message that love was based on our willingness to please and take care of them. Our sense of self became merged with our ability to take care of people, places and things. We began to judge ourselves by a single standard: our ability to be self-reliant and take care of others.

We also became caretakers in order to protect our parents. We came to feel that the only way we could get love was to earn it through caretaking. So we became the "helping hand" that everyone reached out for when they were in trouble, the "listening ear" that was always available.

Freeing Ourselves From The Trap Of Self-Reliance

Many of us have come to rely on having dysfunctional people in our lives because they give us an opportunity to use all the skills we learned in childhood. We gauge our value by how available we are to nurse, feed and support those around us. In many cases our rewards for being the supportive spouse or lover have been verbal or physical abuse.

We convince ourselves to stay in relationships with people who use us because we believe they need us. We use our ability to work without sleep, to handle any situation that comes up or to take abuse as evidence that we are better equipped to take care of everything than anyone else is.

In the end all we are left with are hard feelings. For while those around us want us to take care of them, they also resent us for not allowing them to take care of themselves and for our ability to take care of ourselves. We are caught in an unfulfilling web of resentment and despair created by our willingness to take care of everything and everyone. Our own self-reliance has left us deprived of the nurturing we need.

We rationalize that we are doing our duty, staying loyal even as our hearts break from the sadness around us. We grow used to the hard pain of fear and loneliness and we hide from the truth, the pain of our childhood.

Let us review the relationships that are most significant to us. Let us see how much caretaking we do in our lives. Let us see the impact our compulsive self-reliance has on our lives. In this way we can begin to free ourselves from the trap we are in.

Prepare to invite in your inner child.

Breathe deeply.

Visualize your inner child coming toward you. Let her come close. Ask her to help you make a list of all your significant relationships.

Ask her to help you identify those relationships where you are primarily a caretaker and not a partner, where your compulsive self-reliance defines the relationship.

Write down the list.

Now ask your inner child to tell you how she feels about these relationships and what she would like to change.

Now ask your Higher Parent to help you find a solution to this situation.

Choose one relationship and visualize your Higher Parent guiding you. Ask what you must do to create a more fulfilling life for yourself in this relationship.

Continue this dialogue for each person on your list.

Letting Go Of Compulsive Self-Reliance

As Bill Wilson, the co-founder of Alcoholics Anonymous (AA) said, "AA is no success story in the ordinary sense of the word. It is a story of suffering transmuted, under grace, into spiritual progress." As so it is with us who are trying to transform our co-dependent, compulsively self-reliant behavior into healthy self-affirming behavior.

Letting go is never easy. Giving up self-reliance and placing our trust in a Higher Power goes against every survival instinct known to adult children from dysfunctional families. For us it seems like falling into an abyss when we *let go and let God.*

Letting go feels like dying for some of us. We need to challenge that feeling, to discover we will survive if we learn to let go of control and rely on our Higher Power.

As the old saying goes, "The only way is through." If we are to be free from the dominance of fear, we need to "go through" our feelings.

Let us begin the process of letting go of compulsive self-reliance, of opening our hearts to a power greater than ourselves.

Focus your eyes on a point ahead of you and breathe deeply.

Allow your thoughts to drift to your inner child. See her standing before you.

Imagine yourself and your inner child floating, being carried by your Higher Power.

See yourself letting go and trusting that your Higher Power will take care of you.

When your visualization is finished, write down your experience.

Hard Pain

There are two kinds of pain: hard pain and soft pain. Hard pain is the pain of resistance, the pain we feel when we fight the truth. Hard pain is the pain of fear. Hard pain keeps us stuck in the past.

It is hard for those of us from dysfunctional homes to allow ourselves to experience our feelings of sadness and mourning. We fear we will become overwhelmed by the pain within us and that we will not be able to function. The truth is that our resistance to feeling this pain builds a wall around our heart which, in the end, truly does affect the way we function. The only way through the wall is to work through the feelings.

Soft Pain

Soft pain is the pain of healing. It is the pain of mourning and acceptance. It frees us from the past, allows us to own our feelings and move on with our lives.

Soft pain leads to forgiveness of self and others. We feel the hurt we originally experienced, we resolve it and leave the hurt behind. Soft pain releases our life energy.

Now let us prepare to take a walk through the past, to visit the joy and pain from that time.

We are going to take a walk through your childhood, from infancy through your teenage years. You may want to have available photographs of yourself at various ages to stimulate your memory.

Place a flower on a table or on the floor near you. See that flower. Focus gently on it. Let the beauty and perfection of the flower fill you.

Now visualize your inner child as an infant before you. See her in all her perfection.

Feel her openness, her sense of awe. See your parents as you saw them as an infant. Feel the warmth of your bed; the safety in your mother's touch; the smell of your father's aftershave.

Now move ahead. You are five, running around the place where you lived. See yourself at five. Feel the feelings you had at five.

What was your life like at five? Let your five-year-old tell you how she felt and what she needed.

Now you are 10.

What was life like at 10? Were you happy? What made you happy? Were you already taking care of your siblings and your parents? What did you dream you were going to be when you grew up?

Let your 10-year-old tell you the feelings she had.

Now you are 13.

You have just entered puberty. What was that like?

Was it painful? Were you accepted by your peers? Were you ashamed of your family? Did you hide? What were you looking for when you were 13? What did you need from your parents?

Let your 13-year-old tell you about herself. Open your heart to her.

Now you are 17. Look at yourself at 17.

Perhaps you were in love. What was the beloved like? What does this love feel like? Were you taking care of the one you loved?

What was school like? Were you happy there? What was going on at home?

Let your 17-year-old tell you her hopes, her dreams, her fears. Open your heart and let her tell you what she needed and what she needs from you now.

When you have finished your walk through childhood, write down your experiences at each stage. If you have difficulty writing about a particular time, let your inner child write. You can do this by writing with the hand which is not your dominant hand.

There is only one way to break through the wall of pain inside us and comfort our inner child: that is with the help of our Higher Power. Once we awaken to the reality that we are connected to our Creator, we realize that all things are possible.

Facing God: The Way Out Of Bitterness

When we replaced a belief in a Higher Power with belief in self-reliance, we became God. Because of our fear of depending on anything else but ourselves, we let our hearts grow bitter against God and closed our hearts to God's love.

Bitterness is a poison which kills the best in us. As the well-known minister Harry Emerson Fosdick taught in *Riverside Preachers*, "Bitterness imprisons life; love releases it. Bitterness paralyzes life; love empowers it. Bitterness sickens life; love heals it. Bitterness blinds life; love anoints its eyes."

We need to bring to the surface our resentment and bitterness — to face them and to let them go just as we have our compulsive self-reliance and co-dependent behavior.

It is important to come to terms with disappointment from the past which bred bitterness in our hearts.

Prepare to ask your inner child for help.

Focus on a nearby object and concentrate on breathing deeply.

See your inner child standing before you. Ask her to tell you the disappointment she has faced growing up.

Let her tell you all her resentments.

If she needs to cry, let her and hold her if she needs you to.

Let her give you all her feelings.

When she has finished speaking, write down your experiences.

Our Higher Parent: The Source Of Inner Wisdom

It is important that we learn to reach out and use the wisdom of the Higher Parent in our lives. If we are dealing now with a problem that feels overwhelming or entrapping, it is because we have used only a portion of our inner resources in trying to solve that problem. When we gain access to our Higher Parent, new avenues open and new solutions become apparent.

Let us learn to use our Higher Parent for access to our inner wisdom.

Find a comfortable position.

Focus your eyes on a nearby object and let yourself identify the problem troubling you most right now.

Now visualize a figure dressed in white coming toward you. Identify this figure as your Higher Parent.

Tell your Higher Parent what is troubling you. Listen for the answer.

Let your Higher Parent tell you what you need to do for yourself and your inner child.

Note how you respond to the answer. If you feel yourself resisting your Higher Parent's wisdom, ask your inner child to explain what frightens her. Ask your Higher Parent to help with the fear. Listen for the answer.

Write down all that has transpired during the visualization.

Recovery Is A Spiritual Path

The path to recovery and fulfillment is a spiritual path. Without the help of a power greater than ourselves, we rarely find the strength to take the steps necessary to change our lives. So we stay stuck in the quagmire of pain.

We forget the basic truth about life. We forget that the Creator's plan for us is one of joy and fulfillment, that, in spite of the pain and loss that are part of life, the wonder of life remains.

Our legacy from our Creator is to know relationships where love is given and received, where we are valued and respected and nurtured by one another. Our legacy is to play to the fullest extent our part in the greater plan of creation.

When we do not experience these things in our lives, it is important to remember that we are not victims of fate. We can change what is wrong with our lives. It takes courage and we cannot do it without support but we can do it.

Learning to trust in our Higher Power isn't easy. Learning to use our Higher Parent takes practice. Letting go is one of the hardest things we will ever have to do. But when we let go of our compulsive self-reliance, we free ourselves from the trap of rescuing others and find the energy to rescue ourselves.

When we abandon our caretaking and compulsive self-reliance, we also show respect to those around us. We affirm: "I will take care of you no longer. I respect your wishes to live the way you want to live. I exercise my right to live the way I want to live. This does not diminish my love for you but acknowledges and honors the love I have for myself."

This is God's will for us: to love ourselves; to care for the child within; to move always toward the light. Our Higher Parent hand in hand with our inner child will show us the way if we allow them. The choice is ours.

Remember As Children . . .

We felt the soft pain of healing and went through the feelings.

We gave and expected unconditional love.

We loved ourselves as we were without reservation.

We had free access to our Higher Power.

We reached out and asked for help without shame.

We did not have to be self-reliant in order to have self-esteem.

Guidelines

Recognize that compulsive self-reliance is a learned behavior from childhood. It can be unlearned.

Remember that your self-reliance is only one aspect of who you are. Being vulnerable and needing others is as much a part of you as being self-reliant.

Remember that loving others starts with loving yourself.

Remember that you can have full-well instead of empty-well relationships.

Allow yourself to feel the soft pain of healing instead of the hard pain of resistance.

Learn to reach out to your Higher Parent and use the wealth of inner wisdom always available to you.

Learn that the wisdom of the Higher Parent offers a direct channel to your Higher Power and to trust in the wonder of life.

CHAPTER   4

Accepting How We Have
Learned To Protect Ourselves

Self-Parenting Step 4:

Made an honest assessment of our strengths and weaknesses and accepted the impact our childhood has had upon us as adults.

O! stay thy hand; for yonder is no game.

From **The Faerie Queene** *by Edmund Spenser*

The only way to win is not to play the game.

From the movie **War Games**

*Below my anger must be fear. I don't know. I'm
confused. But I know that my inner child does not
need to worry about this. I just need to figure out
what is going on within me.*

From J.F.'s dialogue with his Higher Parent

Understanding Our Game

A Chinese proverb asserts that "Nobody's family can hang out the
sign, 'Nothing the matter here.'" Most families encounter, "Things that
are the matter." For many of us, these problems and stresses combined
with our families' limited coping skills to produce family dysfunction.

Within our homes, we learned to play "the game" as dictated by our
family rules. We learned what our family expected and, as children
needing love, we usually did what was expected. We learned what
actions were safe and what consequences followed rebellion. Most
importantly, we learned how to protect ourselves. This was how we
learned to approach the world early in life.

Unfortunately, many of us are still playing "the game" we learned at
home. This fact is not lost on those closest to us. We may be accused
of playing games when loved ones cannot get through to us, when
they cannot understand that as a result of a "combat" childhood,
many of us still feel under siege. The war is still raging, if not around
us, then certainly within us.

We continue to play "the game" because in many ways we have
never left home. We recreate our childhood situation in our present
love relationships, in our workplace and perhaps even in our parenting, usually without realizing what we are doing.

We continue to relate to the world as we did when we were children. We see dragons today where we once knew them and we feel compelled to slay them, real or not. We meet enemies today that we first knew when we were very young. Sometimes they even take the guise of loved ones — our spouses, our children — and we feel victimized, powerless, fearful, sad and very angry. We believe we are back in the same situation we so desperately wanted to leave behind.

Life feels discouragingly familiar and we defend ourselves as we did when we were at home. We use the childhood defenses created during the darkness and fear of that time. Even when new ways of protecting ourselves become possible, we do not trust them and continue to use our old defenses. We resist growth, in part because we identify our old familiar defenses as "ourselves" and in part because of loyalty to past ways of doing things.

So we continue to play out the scenarios in which we first performed as children. We may feel betrayed by a superior who is simply a poor manager, trapped by people who really care about us or full of rage at those closest to us. We continually relive the traumas of our childhood in our waking and sleeping lives.

Our task is to make peace now with the old ways we have used to protect ourselves and to move on — to learn new ways to care for our inner child. We begin by looking at our "dark sides," those aspects of ourselves we usually hide, filled, as they characteristically are, with our negative memories, behaviors and impulses. In taking this step, we begin to free ourselves, to become able to learn how to protect ourselves with integrity, with the purpose-filled responses which are appropriate to our lives today.

Beginning At The Beginning

As we begin to look at ourselves we need to understand that all of our actions have roots and that these roots are often found in our childhood experiences. As we look at our defenses, our strengths and our weaknesses, we need to do this with compassion, not only for the person we are today but also for the person we have been. We need to allow compassion for the child within us who dealt as best she could with the problems and tensions she saw. We need to feel this compassion and to embrace it so we may unburden our inner child to allow her to grow, to release her spontaneity, to trust herself and, in so doing, to learn to trust in the world.

By understanding and loving the child that we were, we gain access to the wisdom offered by our Higher Parent. In turn, we can use this wisdom to develop our "light side," that aspect of ourselves that protects us by enhancing us and bringing forth the best that is in us.

Begin by asking your Higher Parent, that part of you which knows the answers and which will gently share them when invited to do so, to help you make a list of the major life events you have experienced.

Make this a list of what has been important to you personally — events such as the death of a puppy, the birth of a brother or sister, a move to a new home. Try to pick at least five events each from your childhood, adolescence, early adulthood and present life. Write down next to each event how you felt at the time.

Allow yourself to think about yourself; see yourself as you write.

Childhood events: **How you felt:**

Adolescent events: **How you felt:**

Early adulthood events: **How you felt:**

Present life events: **How you felt:**

What does this list tell you?

Were the events you remembered mostly happy or mostly sad? Were you afraid in most of them?

Now choose two or three events from your list, including at least one from childhood. Write down how you dealt with each one. Pay particular attention to how you protected yourself, that is, how you dealt with the feelings that came up; how you handled the reactions of your family or friends; what you did the next time a similar event occurred.

What conclusions do you draw from this?

Are you getting a sense that there are certain ways you have protected yourself for a long time? _____ Do these defenses form a pattern? _____ How would you describe this pattern?

Prepare to ask your inner child for assistance.

Allow your eyes to focus on a distant object. Breathe deeply. Invite your inner child to sit on your lap and speak to you.

Ask her to tell you how she feels you protected yourself as a child. Write down what she says, using the hand opposite from your dominant hand.

Ask her to tell you how you protect yourself now.

Ask your inner child to tell you what frightened you most as a child.

How did you protect yourself?

Ask your inner child to tell you what made you the saddest.

How did you protect yourself from the sadness?

Ask your inner child what made you angry.

How did you deal with your anger?

For most of us as children, imitating others was how we learned. We became able to protect ourselves by observing how our mothers, fathers, sisters, brothers, grandfathers or favorite aunts reacted in the same situations.

Again prepare to speak to your inner child.

Focus on a nearby object. Invite your inner child to tell you how the family member most important to you reacted when he or she was sad, angry or fearful.

Write down what she says, using the hand opposite to your dominant hand.

What did you learn from watching your family members react to these feelings?

Ask your inner child to tell you your family's rules about feelings. What feelings were allowed? Were they allowed all the time or just sometimes? If just sometimes, how did you know when it was safe to show your feelings?

Ask your inner child what feelings were disapproved? Were they disapproved all the time or just sometimes? If just sometimes, how did you know when showing them would not be a good idea?

What were the consequences of showing a feeling that was disapproved of?

As a child how did you handle this? What did you feel? What did you show?

Our Masks

As we identify our defenses, we often begin to see patterns, certain ways that we are more likely to respond to what threatens us than others. As we look even more closely, our defenses begin to take shape, sometimes so tangibly they are like masks.

Though we each bring our own unique variations to life experiences, some masks are common. Masks of helplessness say to the world we don't know how to take care of ourselves, that we are dependent, afraid of self-assertion or self-competence. Masks of aggressiveness and compulsive self-reliance allow us to appear so competent that others feel useless around us and they retreat. Masks of perfection allow us to hide our needs, wants, desires, our jealousies, pettiness, vengefulness because we are fearful of our dark sides and the rejection we fear will follow inevitably if our imperfections are revealed.

We can wear masks of calmness when in reality we feel terrified or masks of not caring when what we really fear is what the caring would cost. The list is potentially endless.

We all wear masks. In and of themselves they are harmless. They are merely the outward manifestation of our defenses.

But we can hide our feelings beneath our masks. The key to understanding and making peace with our masks is to identify the feelings they were created to handle. Then we can wear our masks or take them off at will. Then we are in control.

There is a story told by a nine-year-old girl from an alcoholic home which illustrates an important point about masks. She said, "Last night my father came home drunk at 4 a.m. and woke me up, not my mother. He wanted me to make him breakfast. So I got up and made him eggs. I put on my 'I don't care mask' but my inner child was scared."

Her words help us realize that the issue is not whether we wear masks. Our real concern needs to be, "Are we in touch with the feelings beneath the masks?"

Ask your Higher Parent to assist you now in making a list of the masks you wear.

My mask: **Feelings beneath the mask:**

Now prepare to ask your inner child for assistance.

Breathe deeply and invite in your inner child. Look at your favorite mask; show it to your inner child. Ask her how long she has been using this mask. Ask her to remember, if she can, some early incidents involved in the creation of the mask. Write what she says, using your opposite hand.

Ask your inner child how it feels to wear this mask.

Ask her if this is a mask she wants to continue to wear?

Does she see an alternative mask that can be worn?

Close your eyes now and visualize your masks. Choose your favorite and, when you are ready, open your eyes and sketch it on the following page.

Now sketch the face beneath the mask, the face of your feelings, the face of your inner child on the blank page provided.

It may be that the mask you drew suits you well and you do not need an alternative. If you believe this to be the case, move on to the next exercise.

However, if you can think of another way to handle your underlying feelings, allow yourself to develop another mask. This may be one you have been tempted to wear but have not yet tried. Put the new mask on and see how it looks. Allow yourself to be playful and creative. Let your inner child be your guide.

Sketch the mask you would like to wear on the blank page provided.

What does this new mask tell you about yourself?

It may be that you cannot create an image of an alternative mask now. Let yourself come back to this exercise later when the alternative takes shape within you.

Mind-Racing

Mind-racing is a mask we wear on the inside. When we inflict old pain upon ourselves, we create a mask from this confusing pattern.

Mind-racing is the constant replay of events in our minds — variations on "what might have been" — of words we wish we had said, of what we did say, of actions we took, of things we wish we had done or of projections of what someone else may be doing to us right now. Mind-racing is the constant replay of major fears, doubts and insecurities and it often involves themes of jealousy, hurt, rescue and personal risk.

Mind-racing puts us on a road with no exit. Once we are on that road, our thoughts spin ahead in a predictable and painful manner. We know this because we have built the road and traveled it hundreds of times. Mind-racing is a major energy drain for adult children of alcoholic families. It is an ongoing attempt to control the past and the present, to rein in the future using a tight rope of worry and anxiety that paradoxically is one thing we can control.

Reflect on the thoughts or situation that occupies your mind now. Write about this scenario or another from your past that continues to haunt you.

How long has this scenario been playing itself out in your mind?

Do you recognize old themes — for example, your being a victim? Your needing to rescue others while ignoring yourself?

Explore these themes. Think about the role you play in maintaining your own nightmare. Write about these themes.

What unrecognized need of yours is being satisfied by constantly recycling these old themes?

Prepare to ask your inner child for guidance.

Breathe deeply. Close your eyes and see your inner child. Ask her what need she communicates through your mind-racing.

How else can you meet this need? Close your eyes and invite your Higher Parent to speak to you. Write down what he says.

Making An Inventory

"I've got a little list — I've got a little list," wrote W. S. Gilbert and so it is with us all. Each of us has a little, or not so little, list of what might be called character defects, negative traits or even defenses. Whatever we call these aspects of ourselves, committing our list to paper is a means of clarifying how we feel about ourselves. Making such an inventory of both our strengths and our weaknesses is a gift to us and our inner child, for it allows us to document all the ways we protect ourselves.

As well as sifting the past from the present, an inventory is also a tool for helping us live fully in the present. It is a way of acknowledging where we are so we can move on to where we want to be and can be. No inventory can be complete unless we look at both our dark sides and our light sides.

On The Dark Side

It is important to acknowledge our dark sides — our negative traits and characteristics — so that we may understand them and transform them. Our dark sides are the self-protective patterns we maintain, usually at great cost to our inner child. Dark-side behaviors ensure the protection of familiar pain as we attempt to block out old pain we fear we cannot handle. We may even invite attack as a negative form of self-protection. However, the safety of familiar pain doesn't help us feel good about ourselves. Many of us may realize we suffer the loss of self-esteem and hope.

As we complete the inventories of self, we will recognize traits we have documented earlier and begin to realize that our childhood defenses are responsible for much of what we have considered negative about ourselves.

Prepare to list a dark-side trait in the left-hand column that follows and then to list on the right the way this trait protects you. For example, a dark-side trait may be that you mock yourself. The way that this protects you is that it makes you less of a target for the criticism of others. Another dark-side trait might be that you procrastinate, protecting yourself from the risk of success and the changes that success would bring.

Take a moment now and think about how you protect yourself.

Focus on a nearby object. Breathe deeply. Ask your Higher Parent, your voice of internal wisdom, to assist you as you write.

Dark-Side Defense	How It Protects Me

Look At Your Light Side

Our light-side defenses are those that enhance us, those that lead us to our inner light and protect us while not limiting us. These are our positive characteristics; we recognize them because we feel good and strong afterward when we deploy them, not guilty and diminished.

As we make an inventory of our light-side traits, we may recognize strengths from childhood. We will also identify more recently acquired skills that give us assurance and self-esteem. These combined skills allow us to take risks and to feel positive about them.

For example, most of us know how to laugh and, through our laughter, can lighten either our own darkness or that of a friend. Some of us know how to set limits and in so doing can keep others from placing unreasonable demands on us. Some of us can love and be loyal to those we respect, those who are positive forces in our lives and, by doing so, we share our inner child in true intimacy.

The key to understanding whether a defense is light-side or dark-side is how using it makes us feel. Does it enhance us and brighten the light within us? Or does it diminish and keep us in inner darkness?

Take a moment now and think about what you like about yourself. Write in the left-hand column your light-side traits and in the right-hand column how these defenses enhance you.

Ask your Higher Parent to assist you. Focus on a nearby object. Breathe deeply. Listen to what your Higher Parent says and write it down on the following page.

Welcoming The Real You

We all need defenses. As newspapers and newscasters remind us daily, we do not live in a benign world. However, it is important to know when we are defending ourselves and be able to identify the feelings under our masks. It is important to own both our light-side and our dark-side traits. We can have compassion for the dark sides of our natures, knowing we have access to the Inner Light to guide us as we take the risk of change. No one can take anything from us or change us, unless we also wish this. We are the only people who have power over ourselves. When we acknowledge this, we can free our inner child and gain access to our own internal wisdom. We can become integrated and whole at last.

Light-Side Defense   **How It Enhances Me**

Remember As Children . . .

We delighted in knowing how to please others for this was one way in which we showed our love.

We were receptive to how different people expressed their feelings, seeing each new person and each new situation as giving us helpful information on how the world worked.

We felt great self-validation when we could determine how another person felt.

We felt competent when we could care for another and care for ourselves.

We experienced a sense of loss when sources of joy ceased to exist.

We naturally discovered ways to protect ourselves and rejoiced that we were clever enough to do so.

We were naturally strong and resilient.

We enjoyed our strengths and we didn't concern ourselves much with our weaknesses.

Guidelines

Develop compassion for your inner child by understanding the rules of your family.

Allow yourself to know how you developed your childhood defenses.

Be gentle with your inner child as you travel back in time.

Learn to identify the feelings behind your masks.

Take an inventory of your light-side and dark-side traits.

Love both your dark side and your light side for each is part of how you have learned to make sense of the world.

Affirm your inner child daily.

Meditate on the love you have for your entire being.

CHAPTER 5

Intimacy: Letting Go Of Shame

Self-Parenting Step 5:

Learned to share our self-parenting issues with others without self-recrimination or shame.

*Someday, after mastering the winds, the waves, the
tides and gravity, we shall harness for God the energies of love, and then, for a second time in the history
of the world, man will have discovered fire.*

Pierre Teilhard de Chardin

*We could not touch each other. I, your inner child,
made you too vulnerable. It was a crazy world and
being vulnerable meant you would get hurt. I let you
smother me because I wanted to survive. I always
believed in you — that when I was grown up, we
would move out of that circle of defenselessness, fear,
loneliness and anger and we would have power over
our destiny. But you have been powerless as an adult
and I have been filled with rage at you because you
have not set us free.*

Excerpt from K.D.'s letter from her inner child

Love

Learning to love ourselves is the way out of shame, the pathway to
fulfilling relationships, the key to healthy intimacy. For Adult Children
of Alcoholics (ACoAs), learning to trust the heart is one of the hardest
things to do. We have been trained to trust our heads. For those of us
from troubled families, love had a distinctly bittersweet taste.

We were taught, or assumed, as children that the only way to get
love was to earn it. We became the strong ones, the ones who could
take care of everything and needed nothing. Our job was to keep our
parents and other family members from feeling any pain. Love was
defined as something we gave to other people.

We rarely, if ever, paid attention to our needs and nobody else did
either. Our job was to ensure that we hid from our own feelings and
needs and that nobody else saw them. Love for us meant self-
sacrifice. Intimacy was based in being needed, not in being fulfilled.

Our understanding of love was based upon what we saw in our parents' relationships.

Many of us ended up replicating in our present marriages or relationships exactly what we saw in our parents' relationships. Our relationships mirror our self-esteem. If we are in fulfilling relationships, it means we are taking care of ourselves and our inner child. If we aren't, it means we are playing out the shame and self-hatred we learned as children.

Let us prepare to ask our Higher Parent for help.

Clear your mind of any thoughts. Make it an empty vessel.

Visualize your Higher Parent coming toward you with all his wisdom and spirituality. Ask him for help.

Ask your Higher Parent to write you a letter about your parents' relationship.

Ask him to tell you why you are in your present relationship and how it is related to the relationship you saw between your parents.

Now ask your Higher Parent to tell you what you can do to make your present situation a healthy one.

Self-Love: The First Step To Intimacy

As children we learned to live behind a wall of secrecy. It hindered us from being completely honest in our relationships with others and ourselves.

When we were children this may have been wise. Letting our parents know what we really felt and needed could have been dangerous. Since so much of what we wanted and needed seemed to be impossible to attain, we began to submerge our needs and our dreams. We began to lose sight of ourselves at an early age.

Intimacy is sharing who we really are. Most of us have hidden from our real selves. The poet Rilke said love exists "when two solitudes greet and protect one another" — that is, when two people who know who they are fully, give themselves to one another. We cannot share what we do not know.

Let us prepare to face ourselves.

Ask your inner child to help you.

Ask him to tell you who he thinks you are and what you are hiding from yourself.

Using the hand opposite from your dominant hand, write down what your inner child tells you.

Becoming "Self"-Centered

As Albert Schweitzer said, "The tragedy of life is what dies inside a man while he lives." Many of us are living lives in which the best of us is forgotten. We are stuck in situations where our focus is on an alcoholic or a workaholic partner. Or our spouse or lover may be simply self-centered. In any case, our focus is never on ourselves.

Many of us blame our lack of fulfillment on fate, thereby taking ourselves off the hook of accepting responsibility for our own happiness. We walk around as noble victims, while in truth we are only deceiving ourselves. We trade away the truth about ourselves as the price for our dysfunctional relationships and we lose ourselves in the process.

Loving means putting ourselves first in a healthy way. It means facing the hard issues that dysfunctional relationships create, being true to ourselves and honoring our partner's truth as well. It means, if we love an alcoholic, letting her face her disease and not letting it stop us from reaching our own potential.

Loving means being willing to say, "I love you enough to let you decide your own fate and I love myself enough not to let your fate decide my life." It means being willing to say, "I am not a victim. I can take responsibility for my own happiness."

Let us prepare to take responsibility for our lives.

Focus your eyes on a nearby object and breathe deeply.

Now visualize yourself drifting away from your family and friends, drifting until you are alone.
See your inner child come toward you and sit down beside you.

Talk with your inner child. Share with him all the aspects of yourself that you hide from others. Share the part of you that you sacrifice for others.

Write down what you have shared.

Letting Go Of Control

None of us is born a victim. The dysfunctional people in our lives are there because we allow them; they serve a purpose. This is a hard fact for many of us to face but having dysfunctional people in our lives makes us feel that we are still in control. Merely surviving can seem much easier than living fully.

In order to experience life, instead of just surviving it, we need to risk being vulnerable, to let go of some of our control. Most of us hide from the anger and sadness our inner child feels about the way we live. We may find ourselves trying to nurse the entire world back to health while ignoring the needs of our inner child: taking care of others while failing to take care of our inner child.

Let your eyes focus on a nearby object. Breathe deeply and relax.

Ask your inner child to come toward you.

See him clearly.

Ask him to write you a letter letting you know how he feels about the way you ignore him. Do this by writing with your opposite hand.

Self-Honesty

We cannot share with another person if we refuse to see ourselves. We cannot achieve intimacy with someone else until we have achieved intimacy with ourselves.

Facing ourselves will often bring up pain: the pain of disappointment, of dreams seemingly lost, of love grown bitter and futile, of hearts withering without love. But facing ourselves brings a healing pain. This is the pain of recognition that sets us free to affirm our lives.

Let us take an honest look at our past hopes and dreams.

Take a moment. Breathe deeply and let your thoughts drift.

Ask your inner child what you wanted for your life when you were younger, what you wanted to accomplish.

Ask him what you expected your relationships to be like.

Ask him to tell you his dreams.

Let him tell you how he feels about the way you treated those dreams.

When you have finished talking, write down what you both have said.

This is a window into your real self, the self you hide from the world. How do you feel about this part of yourself?

Ask your inner child to write a brief letter to you, telling you how he feels about what you have written.

Write down his answer, using your opposite hand.

Becoming Your Own Hero

We usually get out of life what we expect from it. If we expect little more than abusive relationships, abuse is what we'll get. We can only travel as far as our vision will take us. We cannot exercise options we refuse to see.

Many of us have waited for salvation to come from that knight in shining armor, only to find he never did ride up on his white horse.

We often found someone to worship, to make into a hero and to form a close relationship with, only to be disappointed later by the reality.

We need to become our own heroes. We need to stop looking for others to save us and learn how to save ourselves. We need to take charge of our lives in such a way that we can create options for change.

Prepare now to become your own hero.

Ask your Higher Parent to help you.

Ask this inner voice of wisdom to help you create options for yourself.

Ask this inner voice to show you how to be your own hero.

Write down what you discover.

Shame

Shame is a way of life for many of us, a burden we bear, a secret we keep. In his book, *Bradshaw On: The Family,* John Bradshaw describes a shame-based person as someone who feels inadequate and flawed as a human being; someone who feels what happened to him in childhood was deserved; someone who thinks he is bad and deserves all the bad things that still happen to him. Bradshaw describes a shame-based person as someone who is self-destructive and feels he is almost always wrong.

The feeling of shame goes to the core of our being. As Fossum and Mason in *Facing Shame* write, "While guilt is a painful feeling of regret and responsibility for one's actions, shame is a painful feeling about oneself as a person. Most of all we feel deep within that something is wrong with us."

This feeling of shame can come in a number of different ways: We may feel shame for having survived our childhood and having achieved career success when some of our siblings didn't; we may feel shame for not being able to stop the pain our parents felt; or feel shame at not meeting our parents' expectations.

Feeling Different

Many of us were taught to feel defective as children. Some of us were berated and humiliated by our parents. Others of us felt different because of our circumstances, either because we were brought up in foster homes, adopted or ashamed that our parents were alcoholics. Whatever the reason, somewhere along the way we internalized shame about ourselves. That shame prepared us to accept the abuse that followed in our lives. That shame became the rationale for expecting and getting little for ourselves in life.

Now let us begin to release our inner child from shame.

Lie down on your bed or on a soft couch.

Focus your eyes on a nearby object and breathe deeply.

Hold a pillow and visualize yourself holding your inner child.

Let him tell you his feelings of shame.

Let the tears come if you feel them.

Tell your inner child that your parents were wrong. Tell him he is a good child and that he was not responsible for the bad things that happened — especially if sexual abuse was part of his experience as a child.

Tell him you will protect and love him.

When the visualization is over, write down what you experienced.

Shame And Sex

Often by the time we are adults our sexuality has been totally distorted by the shaming and abuse of our childhood. This affects our present sexual relationships. Enjoyment of sex is difficult for many of us. We have been made to feel bad about our sexuality and have either suppressed our sexual feelings or have allowed others to repeat the abuse of our childhood.

Sex is a good thing. It is a God-given gift. As we watch young children we see the joyful sexuality we are all born with. Sex can open the door to unimagined joy and intimacy. It can be a bridge between two hearts or it can be a hammer we use to beat ourselves and others.

Let us prepare to ask our inner child to help us.

Focus on a nearby object. Breathe deeply. Summon your inner child. See him coming toward you.

Ask him to write you a letter telling you about his sexuality.

Now undress and look in the mirror.

Admire your body.

Slowly touch your body. Allow yourself to feel your sexual feelings.

As you touch each part of your body, repeat this phrase: "My (name the body part) is a gift from God and is meant to be enjoyed."

Do this to your entire body.

When you have completed this, write a love letter to your body and begin to experience the sexual life you want.

Now write down all the negative thoughts you have about your body and your sexuality.

This is the layer of shame you impose on yourself.

Take this list and burn it. As the smoke rises, visualize all the shame and guilt about your sexuality lifting away with the smoke.

In this way we make ourselves empty vessels so the pure sexuality of our inner child can live again. If we allow this to happen, a new world of intimacy and self-love will open up before us and no one can take it away.

When we feel self-acceptance and self-love, we will not allow anyone to abuse us sexually or in any other way. We will be protected from shame. Our sexuality will become a natural expression of love and spirituality. Sex will be a way of speaking heart to heart, soul to soul, inner child to inner child. There will be a oneness and we will feel our life force as the gift it truly is. This is our legacy. We need only to claim it.

Sharing: The Bridge To Intimacy

The way to escape the loneliness and pain of our childhood is by sharing. As children we were taught to keep our feelings and thoughts to ourselves. We were taught that to be open about what was going on at home was to betray our families; being loyal little soldiers, we kept silent about the pain and suffering we were enduring. This became a lifestyle for many of us. We put on a good front for the world while our hearts were breaking.

The way out of shame is to break the old rule of silence. To the extent we still follow childhood's rules, we are still living at home. We have never really left.

Let us prepare to leave home now.

Ask your inner child for help.

Make a list of all the rules about sharing you had as a child.

Look at the list and see how you are continuing the traditions from your childhood in your present life. Decide now to break this negative link with your childhood.

Review the list, creating new traditions for yourself. Write them down next to the old traditions. You have now begun your journey out of shame!

Change will not come easily. We need the strength and guidance of our Higher Parent to be able to free ourselves from the negative, downward pull of our childhood shame. With help from our Higher Parent together with our newfound ability to reach out to others we can break down the walls of pain and create bridges of intimacy and love.

Remember As Children . . .

We experienced our sexuality in all its fullness without guilt.

We had dreams and believed they could come true.

We loved without shame.

We trusted others naturally and believed the best about others and ourselves.

We opened our hearts fearlessly with anticipation and joy.

Guidelines

Take responsibility for your own happiness.

Affirm your right to be free from shame.

Share with others your joy and pain.

Love yourself first.

Allow yourself to see your options and go beyond your sense of self-sacrifice.

Create new personal traditions of self-affirmation.

Practice self-honesty and open the door to true intimacy.

Become your own hero.

CHAPTER 6

Overcoming
Perfectionism

Self-Parenting Step 6:

Became ready to change by giving up the demand to be perfect.

Over these things I could not see;
Theses were the things that bounded me;
And I could touch them with my hand,
Almost, I thought, from where I stand.

Excerpt from **Renascence** *by Edna St. Vincent Millay*

I used to feel that I had to do this inner child thing right. I kept feeling like a failure for my inner child didn't do what other people's inner child did. Then I got it! I mean, I really got it! I was expecting my inner child to act according to some perfect standard. When I realized that, I stopped beating myself up and beating up my inner child. I realized how harsh I am on myself. And in realizing this I have been able to change and to be more, well, gentle.

C.D., sharing her inner child experience

Self-Judgments And Expectations

We often restrict ourselves by making judgments about who we think we should be, how we think we should act, what we think we should receive from each experience, essentially screening out anything new. We limit each potentially new experience to what we can imagine or already know. We do this thinking that we are protecting ourselves, fearing that new experiences will prove overwhelming. We limit ourselves out of loyalty to old ways. We limit ourselves because we are uncertain how to change.

Let us prepare to address our judgments.

Think for a minute about what you expected to receive from Self-Parenting Step 6.

Reread the step and write down your expectations.

Now draw a circle completely around what you have written. Attach a squiggly string coming down from it. Take a brightly colored pencil or crayon and shade in the word-filled circle.

Look at what you have written, drawn and colored. Imagine it to be a balloon, a bright, helium-filled balloon. Imagine holding the expectation-filled balloon by the string and feeling it tug at your hand. Now let it go. Close your eyes and visualize your balloon gently drifting away.

While it is important to have expectations, it is equally important not to be ruled by them. As you now proceed with your inner child work, note your expectations, allow respect for them, then gently let them go as you would a helium-filled balloon. In this way, you can ensure that your new experiences are not viewed only through the lens of your past.

Coming To Terms With Our Need For Perfection

Often our perfectionism is just a form of self-protection, a way of controlling ourselves so we will be more acceptable to others. Particularly for adult children from dysfunctional families, our need for perfection is often the result of the child in us deciding that "If only I could _____ (fill in the blank), then things at home would get better."

Many of us grew up seeing ourselves as both the cause and the solution to the nameless tensions and problems we experienced in our families. This led to us seeing ourselves as in control. To admit otherwise would have been terrifying, for we feared facing the fact no one was in control. To avoid this painful reality, we chose to behave in our families as if it were our responsibility to hold things together by doing everything "just right." We believed that if we set the table "just right," the rages would not begin at dinner. We decided that if we cared for our mother perfectly, our father would not be able to hurt her. We felt that if we succeeded, our parents would experience pride and give up their self-loathing.

This need for control and perfection became part of our identity and many of us carry this need into our adult lives, often with confusing results. We may continue to try to shield others from their pain, without understanding or even trying to understand the source of their pain. We continue to sacrifice ourselves in our effort to please others perfectly. And, we may also find ourselves attempting to make loved ones live up to our impossibly high standards. We expect perfection from them and can be angry and take revenge when they falter.

Let us prepare to ask our Higher Parent for assistance.

Focus on a nearby object. Clear your mind and begin to breathe deeply.

Ask your Higher Parent to help you list all the situations you encounter in life where you try to perform perfectly.

Prepare to ask your inner child for assistance now.

Choose two situations from the list you've just written. Frame some questions for your inner child. How old were you when you began to expect self-perfection in each and every situation? Ask how you achieved perfection in these areas when you were a child.

Take a deep breath, close your eyes and invite in your inner child.

Ask your questions and write down what she says, using the hand opposite from your dominant hand.

Now ask your inner child, "What were you afraid would happen if you were not perfect?"

Ask your inner child, "What did being perfect in these situations protect you from?"

Ask your inner child if she still feels the need to be protected in this way.

Celebrating Our Differences

Celebrating our specialness is one way we can make peace with our need for perfection. From birth, each of us has possessed "one of a kind gifts" that result in our being uniquely different from each other.

By recognizing and owning our specialness, we can learn to celebrate it. It may be, for example, that we sing enthusiastically and delightfully off-key; we may walk heavily or have large hands; or we may have kinky curly red hair, lovely slanted eyes or dark velvety skin. We may even have extremely interesting character lines in our faces and subtle gray highlights in our hair.

We are each special, just as the Creator intended. We are each unique. Not one of us came from a used mold. As well as being unique, we are also each perfect, perfectly wonderful!

Prepare to meet your inner child now.

Breathe deeply and allow your focus to soften.

Let your thoughts be of how you look now, of how you are in the world.

Ask you inner child to help you list your special qualities. Write them down.

My Special Qualities

Read over the list. What does this tell you about yourself? Do you like the package you see now?

Preparing For Change

For many of us, our need for perfection is tied in with our fear of change. Change — inviting in the unknown — can, in view of our past, be a frightening burden. We may feel compelled to change and at the same time feel inadequately prepared to do so. Feeling burdened in such a way can elicit anger and we can hesitate about trying to do what we do not know how to do perfectly.

We can make peace with all of these feelings by embracing them and by realizing that, as Joseph Joubert wrote, "Children need models more than they need critics." Our inner child needs to be encouraged not only to seek out new models for change, but also to recognize how much she already knows about this process.

We all have witnessed change in ourselves and in our families. We have seen models for change that have not worked and others which have brought about desired results. Change may not be as new to us or as unknown as we think.

Let us prepare to ask our Higher Parent, our inner voice of wisdom, to assist us.

Focus on a nearby object. Breathe deeply.

Ask your Higher Parent now to help you make a list of changes you have made. Let him guide you as you think about your personal life, your close relationships, your daily affairs, your work life. Choose examples from as many areas as are available and comfortable. Write down what your Higher Parent says.

Changed from:	Changed to:

Choose two examples from your list.

Ask your Higher Parent these questions:

"How did I know I needed to change?"

"How did I know where to begin?"

"What barriers did I need to overcome?"

"How did I overcome these barriers?"

Changing

"Whatever you can do, or dream you can, begin it," wrote the poet, Goethe. Changing is, after all, a matter of having a vision and allowing ourselves the courage to act on that vision. It is important that we allow ourselves to dream and let thoughts of our changed selves be part of our vision.

We have been listing changes we have already experienced in our lives, many of them of our own choosing and of our own making. Looking at this list may not suddenly make change easier but it does help us recognize that we have definitely established ways of making changes. Each of us has developed internal road maps that help us move things about in our lives.

Many of us, however, can identify an additional struggle, that of learning to welcome change and to accept all the feelings — fear, anger and excitement — that accompany it. It helps to realize that change is seldom absolute. Usually change is a process; it can be a little or a lot, backward or forward, in a straight line or in a curve.

It is usually only by experience that we learn just what the best choices are for us. We may find we don't like the result of a particular change and try another. Sometimes a change results in a greater appreciation of a previous circumstance and we choose to return to it. It is important to realize we have free will. We can move again or make new choices if it feels right to do so.

Change means allowing our inner child to experiment, viewing those parts of our lives that we wish to change as opportunities to learn, through trial and error, what is right for us. Change gives us opportunities to act freely, letting our inner child be spontaneous and curious about the world. Change involves allowing our inner child to be messy, as children naturally are, allowing her to start and stop, without perfect order or design.

Change asks us to trust that, as we seek so we will find and recognize what we need. We simply need to allow the process of change to begin, allowing ourselves to be guided by our inner child, our spontaneity, and our Higher Parent, our internal wisdom. Using their innate abilities we can make the best choices for ourselves.

Let us prepare to invite our inner child in now.

Focus your eyes on a point near you. Breathe deeply.

Ask your inner child what you need to change. Talk with her about what you need to do today and write down what she says.

Ask your inner child how you need to prepare for this change. What experiments do you need to do to determine your options?

Ask her how you can make this change safely.

Ask her how you will know if this is the right decision.

Ask her what you will continue to need to do to take care of yourself as you make this change.

Now prepare to ask your Higher Parent to assist you.

Clear your mind and distance yourself from what you just wrote. Focus on a distant point and let your thoughts drift.

Now read over your notes from your dialogue with your inner child. Writing any additions with a differently colored pencil or pen, ask your Higher Parent to suggest helpful steps in the process you have identified. For example, if your inner child has said you need support to make a change, ask your Higher Parent to help you identify who can offer this support, knowing that your inner wisdom will supply the answers you need.

The Path Least Taken

"If I didn't start painting, I would have raised chickens." This is how Grandma Moses described the choices she saw in her life. We each have such choices. Change sometimes involves the unexpected and sometimes not. Change is part of our lives. We can learn to allow ourselves to greet it, to know it and to love ourselves through it.

Remember As Children . . .

We knew ourselves to be perfect.

We delighted in our specialness and took pains to make sure others noticed it.

We delighted in doing things differently.

We loved to experiment in seeing how things worked — holding our cups in different ways, even if it meant we spilt our juice!

We enjoyed our messes. Usually they meant we had tried something new.

Change was the order of the day. Our lives were focused on change and we were growing and changing every minute.

Guidelines

Own your self-judgments and expectations for they will tell you much about yourself.

Be prepared, however, not to filter all your experiences through your self-judgment and expectations in order to avoid recreating only what you know.

Allow yourself to know what you feel you need to do perfectly, so you can move beyond this and live uniquely.

Create safe harbors as you contemplate change.

Learn to love and embrace your uniqueness as the Creator's special gift to you.

CHAPTER 7

Becoming Part Of
The Family Of Man

Self-Parenting Step 7:

Learned to embrace our uniqueness and connectedness to others in a spirit of love and humility.

Only one thing takes us straight to the Almighty, to the inner experience, and that is humility. Letting go of the hard shell of the ego gives the true experience of God. When there is humility, there is love; and where there is love, there is humility.

Gurumayi Chidvilasananda

I am so tired of always trying to beat everyone else. My life is constant competition. I'm always jealous when someone gets more recognition than me. I feel so separate from everyone else; I know we are all God's children but I don't feel that way. Please help me to let go of my fear, my need to be better than everyone else. Please help me to find a way to feel my love for my brothers instead of my anger. Please help me to feel more humility instead of my pride.

Excerpt from F.D.'s letter to his Higher Power

Humility

Humility is the acceptance of reality. It is the acknowledgment of the truth about ourselves. It is accepting the truth of a situation whether we like it or not. Humility is accepting a flat tire rather than railing at our fate. Humility is accepting a compliment. Humility is admitting when we are wrong. Humility is knowing we all fit into God's plan equally and are no better nor worse than anyone else.

Humility is the great stabilizer. When we are humble, we are uninvolved with our egos. When we are humble, we are as one with each other. Our egos lead us to view ourselves as better or worse than others and keep us stuck in competitive jealousy. The way out of the ego trap is to make ourselves consciously aware of the ways in which we build ourselves up or pull ourselves down.

Let us prepare to speak to our inner child.

Clear your mind of everyday thoughts. Breathe deeply and invite your inner child in.

On a separate sheet of paper make a list of all the ways you put yourself down.

Let your inner child help you.

Ask your inner child how he feels about the list.

Using the opposite hand to your dominant hand, let him write you a letter about his feelings.

Comparing

As Carl Jung said, "Nothing exerts a stronger psychic effect upon the human environment, and especially upon children, than the life which the parents have not lived." Many of us have felt forced to live out the unfulfilled dreams of our parents.

Often this takes the form of competition among siblings. As children, many of us were compared by our parents to our siblings or other children. This constant comparison has become a way of life for many of us. It has left our self-esteem dependent upon being better than others. Now these acts of comparison have become almost unconscious, something we do automatically.

Let us prepare to assess how much we live by comparison.

Clear your mind and breathe deeply.

Let yourself relax. See your Higher Parent coming toward you.

Ask your Higher Parent, your inner wisdom, to help you make a list of all the areas of life in which you compare yourself to others.

Now ask your inner child how he feels about this list.

Write down what you discover from this exercise.

No Better Nor Worse Than Anyone Else

As young children, we were completely self-affirming and self-accepting. Until we learned differently, we had no need to compare ourselves to others. We took joy in the achievements of others and didn't feel diminished if another person could do something we couldn't. We were born naturally humble, accepting ourselves and others as we were.

As we grew, we were taught that we had to be more or less than others. We were taught that we were not good enough as we were. We developed a false sense of ourselves.

Many of us mistake self-deprecation for humility. We think if we put ourselves down, it proves we are not proud. That is a misconception.

The focus remains on us even while we are putting ourselves down. When we put ourselves down and make ourselves worse than everyone else, we are still separating ourselves from other people, saying we are better at being worse than anyone else. We are taking pride in how terrible we are.

On the other side of the coin are those of us who believe we are special because we come from dysfunctional homes and we have suffered. Many of us believe that the childhood skills we developed to survive in our families have made us superior to people who did not go through what we did.

In either case, we are caught in the trap of false pride and false humility. The way out is to make an honest assessment of ourselves as no better nor worse than anyone else.

Let us prepare to accept ourselves as we really are.

Focus on a nearby object and breathe deeply.

Ask your Higher Parent to help you.

See her standing before you. Let her come toward you.

Ask her to help you make a list of your assets and deficits.

Now review the list and check those areas you feel particularly bad about and also the areas that make you feel superior.

Ask your Higher Parent to help you let go of your need to make yourself feel better or worse about the items on your list.

Let her answer you with a letter.

God Does Not Make Junk

To accept that God does not make junk is the same as accepting ourselves as valuable people, just the way we are and accepting that the childhood messages were wrong. It is our hurt, frightened, rejected inner child who leads us to reject ourselves.

Our inner child does not trust that he will be loved and valued unless the game of better or worse is continued. This game is all our inner child knows. It is up to us to change that. With the help of our Higher Parent, we can learn to set limits on our inner child's false need to puff himself up or put himself down.

Prepare now to help your inner child cope with his feelings of inadequacy.

Make yourself comfortable and breathe deeply.

See your inner child before you. Ask him to share his feelings about himself with you.

Ask him to tell you how he feels when he compares himself to others.

Ask him to tell you of his fear that he will be diminished by the successes of others.

Write down what he says.

Now let your Higher Parent answer your inner child.

Breathe deeply and focus on a nearby object.

Let your Higher Parent write your inner child a letter telling him what he needs to hear in order to become self-validating.

Remember we are all unique. We are all different. But we are not better nor worse than one another. It is important to embrace our uniqueness, to validate all that we are but it is also important to remember that being all we can be does not need to diminish anyone else. Conversely, someone else being all he can be does not diminish us.

Recovery — Connecting To Others In The Spirit Of Love

As Dr. Christiaan Barnard said, "Suffering isn't ennobling, recovery is." All too often we think we are getting better because we are in touch with our pain. In fact some of us believe that the more pain we feel, the closer we are to recovery.

This is not the case. Recovery is about joining the family of man. It's about learning to share our love with others. When we break down the walls between ourselves and others by practicing humility, we join the human community and leave behind the isolation and mistrust of our childhood.

Recovery is about feeling our joy. Recovery is about learning to live in the present and leaving the past behind. It is about embracing our oneness with each other.

It is about remembering that no task is greater than any other, no job more important than any other, no race or religion better than any other.

It is about being brothers and sisters to one another.

Let your focus soften on a nearby object.

See your inner child coming toward you.

Bring him close to you.

Tell him that he is enough as he is. Tell him he is lovable and perfect as he is.

Let him answer you.

Write his answer down.

Now let your Higher Parent respond to your inner child.

Let your source of inner wisdom guide you.

Write down the guidance you receive from your Higher Parent.

We are in charge of our choices. It is up to us to decide to let go of our need to compare. If we can do this, we can become humble without putting ourselves down. We can accept our place in the world without struggling to enhance ourselves. Then we can embrace our uniqueness and share our love with our brothers and sisters.

As the theologian William Sloan Coffin said, "The world is too dangerous for anything but truth and too small for anything but love." When we recognize that living honestly and sharing our love are the keys to true humility, the path to serenity and true fellowship will be open to us.

Remember As Children . . .

We had no need to compare ourselves to others.

We were self-validating.

We didn't need to be better than someone else to feel good about ourselves.

We took joy in other people's accomplishments.

We felt our pain and joy naturally and didn't get stuck in either feeling.

We were born naturally humble.

Guidelines

Recognize that comparing yourself to others will only work against you.

Allow yourself to make an honest appraisal of yourself as being no better nor worse than you really are.

Create a bridge between you and your brothers and sisters by sharing your love as well as your pain.

Accept your uniqueness as your gift from God, a gift which makes you different but not better than anyone else.

Affirm yourself as being as perfect and lovable as you are.

Look for the similarities rather than the differences between yourself and others.

Allow yourself to make yourself conscious of all the ways you put yourself down.

Affirm that God doesn't make junk — that all people are of equal value regardless of their station in life.

CHAPTER 8

Learning
Self-Forgiveness

Self-Parenting Step 8:

Learned self-forgiveness and made amends to our inner child.

Love never ends.

I Corinthians 13:8

*I realized the more I allowed myself to love myself,
the less I wanted to punish myself. So simple. I see
options now, options my family didn't see, so they
couldn't lead me to them. I now put my energy into
figuring out how I can resolve a problem, even if I
caused it, rather than being stuck in beating myself
up all the time. I really feel free.*

D.G., after taking the 8th Step

Loyalty And Options

As Alexander Pope wrote in his *Moral Essays,* "Just as the twig is
bent the tree's inclined," so we first learn how to function in the world
from our families. From them, we learn how to define problems and
how to identify alternatives. We learn how to respond and how to
hide. We loyally continue these old ways of dealing with the world
into our adult lives. This serves to bind us to our families, to identify
ourselves with them and to behave according to their standards. Such
identifications can be good.

An important aspect of recovery is being able to recognize what we
want to keep, what enhances us, while separating out what we need
to own but leave behind because it diminishes us. Loyalty to dysfunctional family traditions, traditions which do not work, limits and hurts
us. Such loyalty condemns us to repeat the same dysfunctional patterns. At the same time, trying to give up these old unworkable
traditions can be wrenchingly painful. We feel separated from our
families, alone, unsupported and frightened.

Let us prepare now to enlist the help of our Higher Parent.

Clear your mind by focusing on a nearby object and breathe deeply.

SELF-PARENTING 12-STEP WORKBOOK

Turn your thoughts to your Higher Parent. Ask this wise inner voice to identify your family traditions concerning:

Guilt — When should you feel it? How should you show it?

Responsibility — How should you show responsible behavior? How did your family respond when members did not meet their responsibilities?

Clear your mind. Allow your Higher Parent to come close to you and guide your thoughts.

Ask your Higher Parent to help you list those behaviors or qualities you react to and thus give them power over you; those behaviors and qualities you allow to drain you of energy and time. Next to each behavior, write the word that shows the judgment you make on it; for example, "stupid," "hateful," "mean," "hurtful," "thoughtless."

What do your judgments of others tell you about yourself? What are you most sensitive to in others?

Releasing Ourselves And Others — Forgiveness

"Is it possible to forgive?" we may ask, when all we can remember is the pain, the rage, the vain wish that we could relive certain moments, change them, make them better or erase them. Our energy becomes bound up in these conflict-creating memories and the tension hounds us in our daily lives. We are tense whenever certain names are mentioned, whenever we think of particular places or stages of our lives. Such tension drains us and we cannot know rest or peace.

Our Higher Parent can help us rationally perceive life's events as neutral. Our Higher Parent can help us begin to put space between hurtful events and our reaction to them. Also, our Higher Parent can help us gain understanding so that we do not feel so helplessly consumed by our memories.

We should regard forgiveness as making space within us so that we may eventually replace with love the pain and rage which have driven us. Forgiveness is largely about seeing more in others than just their actions.

Let us prepare to invite in our inner child.

Ask your inner child to tell you how she feels about each of the following things. Write down what she says.

Guilt:

Responsibility:

Forgiveness:

Self-forgiveness:

Forgiveness — How was it shown? Under which conditions?

Self-forgiveness — How was it shown? Under which conditions?

Now prepare to enlist the support of your inner child.

Ask your inner child which of these traditions you are still following.

Ask her how this feels.

Breathe deeply now and focus on a point just in front of you.

What choices do you have when people behave in ways that arouse these judgmental feelings in you? Make a list of them.

Breathe deeply now. Review the list you have just completed and allow yourself to experience your judgmental feelings. Write down how it is to experience these feelings.

Prepare to ask your inner child for assistance now.

Choose one or two of your judgments of others. Ask your inner child to tell you if these reactions have been part of you for a long time, perhaps from adolescence or childhood. See if you can remember an incident in your childhood which resulted in your judging someone in this same way. How did you react then? Are you reacting the same way now?

Breathe deeply. Focus on a nearby object.

Allow your inner child to speak to you about the roots of your judgments.

Write down what she says.

Ask your inner child what you want to specifically forgive in someone else. Ask your inner child if you are truly ready to forgive the person or persons involved in this hurtful situation.

Now take a deep breath. Allow your thoughts to turn to this event.

Now write down all the details of the situation for which you want to forgive someone else. Listen to what your inner child tells you.

Write down all the feelings you experienced during the event.

Take your time. Allow yourself to experience these feelings as they arise.

When you have finished, read through what you have written. Ask yourself if you are still willing to forgive.

If your answer is yes, mark an *X* through your description of this event, and write at the bottom that you have forgiven _____ for this event now and forever. Develop an affirmation concerning this event, allowing you and those you have forgiven to go on in peace.

When you think of this event in the future, let yourself remember it is forgiven and that you need to spend no further energy dealing with it.

Again prepare to invite in your inner child.

Ask her how it feels to forgive this person for this act.

Breathe deeply now and write down what she says.

If you have found you cannot forgive, it is important to realize that your feelings and energies are still so bound up in the event you have described that you cannot honestly free yourself from your feelings. Love yourself; do not judge yourself. Accept your feelings, even though you may wish you could be free from the hurt you are experiencing in harboring them. Try this exercise again, later on, when you feel it is the right time to do so.

Making Amends To Others

Often when it is time to make amends to others, we seize up. We may feel so worthless and fearful that we believe we can never possibly make amends. The first step is simply to let others know we regret our actions as well as the unfortunate consequences our actions have caused. At the same time, we need to recognize the impact that our actions have had on us. We need to allow ourselves to learn from what we have done, so we may have the option of change in our daily lives.

Let us prepare to ask our Higher Parent for assistance now.

Choose something you have done for which you would like to make amends. Your action can involve a co-worker, a lover, a child or other family member.

Focus on a nearby object. Breathe deeply and ask your Higher Parent to tell you what resources you can use to make amends.

Write down what your Higher Parent says.

Now ask your inner child for assistance.

Breathe deeply and focus on an object in front of you.

Now ask your inner child which option for making amends feels the best to her. Ask her how she thinks she'll feel when she makes amends.

Ask her to make a firm plan to make amends within a certain period of time. Ask her to set this time.

How does this feel?

Making Amends To Our Inner Child

As Aesop said, "A crust eaten in peace is better than a banquet partaken in anxiety." This is an important lesson to remember as we travel the road of self-forgiveness. Forgiving ourselves and making amends to our inner child begins with accepting a crust of bread in peace and then another and then another. Self-forgiveness is a process, a trusting acceptance that we will be fed, not satiated; that we will have our immediate hungers met while the needs of tomorrow will be filled as they occur.

Achieving inner peace involves recognizing that many of our beliefs about our power in the world are based on our childhood experiences. Those of us who lived in dysfunctional homes have not yet learned how to grow beyond these childhood experiences. We have not learned how to grow through self-parenting.

Our inner child needs a guide to lead her through the painful experiences she has known; someone to hold her safely by the hand and teach her how to walk through the world; someone to love her unconditionally and accept her; someone to show her that her childhood's beliefs need no longer apply; someone to show her she is more than a remembered hurtful or shameful action.

We can be this loving, liberating guide for ourselves.

First, we need to realize that our inner child's self-blame consumes the energy that we need to follow our inner guide. Finding peace must begin with forgiveness.

Let us prepare to invite in our inner child.

Prepare to write what she says to you, using the hand opposite from your dominant hand.

Now allow your thoughts to drift to your inner child. Focus on a point nearby and breathe deeply as you allow her to come close and sit in your lap.

Ask your inner child to tell you what she wants to be forgiven for doing — or not doing. Ask her to tell you what crime she committed: what needs she did not meet, what needs she overlooked. Was her *crime* that of being a child in a situation where an adult's presence was needed? Ask her to tell you the things for which she needs to be forgiven. Write down what she says.

Review what you have written. Ask yourself if you are now ready to help your inner child release this memory. If so, mark a large *X* through this memory. Allow yourself to realize that if this memory should come to you again, your inner child has been forgiven and the self-punishment can stop.

Write now on the bottom of your inner child's statement an affirmation such as, "I forgive my inner child — myself — for this now and forever. I release my inner child — myself — to enjoy a more loving acceptance of my entire being."

Prepare to speak to your inner child once more.

Ask her how it feels to be released.

Breathe deeply and write down what she says.

If you find that you still cannot allow forgiveness, accept this as an important piece of information about yourself and about your "unfinished" business with your past. Do not blame yourself if the time is not right now. You may want to try this exercise again later. You will know when the right time occurs.

Creating Our Own Reality

"To be what we are, and to become what we're capable of becoming, is the only end of life," said Robert Louis Stevenson.

In many ways self-parenting is about coming to terms with the truth that we are each responsible for much of the reality that we choose to live in. We can each choose how we react to the events of our lives, either the actions of another person or our own actions. We can choose how much importance we place on what a family member or friend has just said to us. We can choose how much time we allow to elapse between an injury we created and our attempt to set it right.

We can choose. The reality of this freedom allows us great power and an opportunity for an even greater love for ourselves and those around us.

Remember As Children . . .

We freely forgave ourselves for our errors.

We said, "Sorry," and meant it and did not feel the worse for it.

We existed within a space of peace.

We loved ourselves no matter what we did.

We loved ourselves no matter what other people did to us.

Guidelines

Know that you are free to develop your own traditions.

Allow yourself to experience your capacity for forgiveness.

Own your power to create self-forgiveness.

Realize your capacity for creating your own reality.

CHAPTER 9

The Promises Of
Self-Parenting

Self-Parenting Step 9:

Healed our inner child by realizing the promises of self-parenting in our daily living.

Life was meant to be lived, and curiosity must be kept alive. One must never, for whatever reason, turn his back on life.

Eleanor Roosevelt

I want to thank you for all the gifts that you have given me. I try to be appreciative and share my gifts but at times I don't. I'm annoyed at myself for not having utilized or [outright refused] some of the gifts. Please help me to keep trusting you and remain faithful to you.

Excerpt from G.S.'s letter to his Higher Parent

Claiming The Promises Of Recovery

Most of us have lived reactive lives. We have let circumstances dictate how we live. If we felt good about ourselves but those around us were experiencing problems, we would forgo our happiness to experience their pain.

Realizing the promises of self-parenting in our everyday lives means consciously holding on to the benefits of our self-worth despite the conditions of those around us. This is not always easy but it is necessary if our inner child is to know true healing.

Let us review where we stand with the promises of recovery.

Abundance

When we self-parent, we take responsibility for meeting our own needs. We do not allow ourselves to be dependent on others for fulfillment. We let ourselves enjoy life's gifts, free of the guilt and shame we have been programmed to feel since childhood.

When we realize this promise, we move away from a poverty mentality, unable to enjoy life in its fullness, into a consciousness of prosperity. We challenge our parents' views of the world and create new possibilities for ourselves and our children.

Let us make an abundance inventory.

Clear your mind by focusing on a nearby object and breathe deeply.

Ask your Higher Parent to help you assess all the gifts in your life.

Take a moment now and write down all the ways you recognize there being abundance in your life.

Review the list. Consider the range of God's gifts to you. Now record those things you would like to add to your life's abundance. Make a commitment to yourself to bring them into your life.

Intimacy

Our inability to know satisfying relationships with our spouses, lovers or friends is a source of great despair for many of us. Our co-dependent behavior diminishes our capacity for intimacy.

As we self-parent, we tear down walls and let people in. We break out of our isolation to join the human family. The promise of intimacy is the key that opens the door to loving, satisfying relationships.

Focus on a nearby object and allow yourself to relax.

Invite your inner child to sit beside you. Ask him to visit the relationships in your life with you.

Identify those relationships in which you share who you really are.

Make a list of all these relationships.

Ask your inner child how you can add to this list.

Write down what he says you need to do to grow in intimacy.

Manageability

This is the gift of sanity. When we give up our addiction to control, we take ourselves out of the driver's seat and let our Higher Power organize our lives. Restoring manageability in our life means taking care of our needs and responsibilities in a healthy way.

Let us see where we stand with regard to manageability.

Make a list of the areas of unmanageability in your life.

Now invite your Higher Parent to help you to restore order and manageability to your life.

Let your thoughts drift. Ask your Higher Parent, your inner wisdom, to write you a letter telling you what you need to do.

Now review your Higher Parent's letter and make a daily commitment to work at following her guide to sanity and manageability in your life.

Living In Today

For too long we have missed the joy of the present because of the pain of the past. We carry our childhood trauma into our present relationships and we use our childhood defenses to protect ourselves. The promise of self-parenting is that we can live in the present.

We achieve this by attending to our inner child when he needs us, calming his fears, protecting him from harm and making sure he feels loved. In these ways we process the past and live in the present.

Let us prepare to have a dialogue with our inner child.

Breathe deeply and focus on a point just ahead of you.

Invite your inner child to come before you and tell him from now on you will take care of him. Tell him you will be the parent; he will be the child.

Let him know you each need to live in the present.

Let him respond by writing you a letter. Write his words with the hand opposite to your dominant hand.

Daily attention to the parenting needs of your inner child will bring realization of the promise of living in the present, free of childhood fear.

Self-Definition And Autonomy

Self-parenting means becoming autonomous. It means defining ourselves according to our own needs and desires, not by the needs of others. It means letting go of the need for repeating chaos in our lives. It means no longer accepting the role of victim but being instead the author of our own scripts, writing our own roles in life.

Breathe deeply. Ask your Higher Parent to help you list those life areas where you still feel like a victim.

Now review the list and write down how you maintain each situation.

Ask your Higher Parent to help you take charge of your life in these areas.

Healthy Family Traditions

When we self-parent and break out of the rigid repetition of old dysfunctional patterns, we learn to take risks and make choices. Working to realize the promise of healthy family traditions allows us to rebirth into a self-affirming way of life.

Focus on a nearby object. Ask your Higher Parent to help you make a list of all the new traditions you have created for yourself and your family.

Review this list. It is your personal map to an abundant life. Keep adding to it. Let it be your gift of health to yourself and your family. Let a new self-affirming, spiritually-based lifestyle be your legacy to the next generation.

Unconditional Self-Love

This is perhaps the greatest promise, that we can return to our original childhood condition of self-love and self-acceptance. This is the path to freedom. When we claim this promise, we no longer hurt ourselves and no longer accept abuse from others.

Breathe deeply. Invite your inner child to come to you and help you list the areas in which you need to practice self-acceptance and self-love.

For each area listed, write a specific response you can make which will allow you to transform your present self-judgment into unconditional self-love.

For instance, if you judge yourself harshly for your imperfection in a certain area of life, write a plan outlining how you will achieve self-acceptance in it. Now make a personal commitment to work through the steps of this plan on a daily basis.

Claiming Our Spiritual Selves

This is the promise of serenity. In this promise we claim our true nature, as in the old saying,

That we are not human beings sharing our spiritual experience,
But spiritual beings sharing our human experience.

Prepare to ask your Higher Parent for help in completing a spiritual inventory.

Breathe deeply. Ask your Higher Parent to guide you in listing all the practices that enhance your spirituality.

Now write a letter to your Higher Parent asking for help with your spirituality.

Let your Higher Parent write a response.

Remember when you claim this promise, nothing can really hurt you again.

Freedom From Guilt

In self-parenting we learn to correct situations when they occur, rather than letting bad feelings build up. We choose not to allow ourselves to be burdened with guilt. We move beyond the feelings, making the choice to repair bad situations rather than reliving them.

Make a list of all the things you feel guilty about on a separate sheet of paper.

Now burn the list.

Watch it go up in smoke and as the smoke rises, allow your guilt to leave you and drift away with it.

The Grace Of Forgiveness

Forgiveness creates a bridge from heart to heart. Harboring resentments hurts us more than the people we resent. Hate poisons our hearts and spirits. When we hold on to hate and resentment, we lose our ability to open our hearts to ourselves and to others. Forgiveness unlocks the doors and allows us access to our love.

Ask your inner child to help you make a list of the people toward whom you harbor hate or resentment.

Now visualize yourself inviting each of these people into your heart.

See your heart filling with light. Come close to each person you have invited in and place that person in the light.

Committing yourself to this practice will eventually relieve you of your burden of hate and allow you to know the grace of forgiveness.

Amends To Our Inner Child

Forgiving others is only part of the journey. Ultimately the most important person to forgive is ourself. When we claim the promise of self-forgiveness, we reveal our love for our inner child and free him from his history of pain.

Soften your focus by looking at a nearby object. Let your consciousness drift.

See your inner child. Let him come close.

See how much he needs love, acceptance and forgiveness.

Hold him tight. Let him know you forgive him. Let him know that no matter what happens, you will always forgive him.

When you have finished talking to your inner child, write down what you have experienced.

List areas where you have already made amends to your inner child.

List the areas that still remain.

Claiming this promise of self-forgiveness leads us to an inner world of warmth, self-love and self-acceptance. Claim it now!

Shame And Trauma Lifted Away

The final promise is freedom from shame and trauma, the twin chains of our oppression. Self-parenting is our defense against shame. We are able to let go of the pain of childhood and we are able to make sense of our childhood traumas, resolve them and leave them behind.

Visualize your inner child. Ask him to sit on your knees. Look into his face.

Tell him that you are taking away the shame from his past. Tell him that he no longer has to struggle, that he is free to play. Tell him he is a good child and that, no matter what has happened in the past, he is the most lovable and wonderful child in the world.

Recite these words like a mantra.

Afterward, write down what you have experienced.

This visualization, this mantra, can be a daily affirmation, your key to realizing the promise of freedom from shame and trauma.

Remember As Children . . .

We were naturally self-affirming.

We expected our days to be filled with joy and wonder.

We expected success.

We were constantly curious about life and saw life as an adventure.

We believed we were perfect as we were.

We accepted ourselves even when we made mistakes.

Guidelines

We need to safeguard our positive feelings, even when those we love are in pain.

Sharing our true identity is the key to intimacy.

When we let go of our addiction to control, we allow our Higher Power to organize our lives.

When we meet the parenting needs of our inner child, we are freed from childhood fears.

Forgiveness creates a bridge from our hearts to the hearts of those who have hurt us.

Making sense of our childhood shame and trauma lets us leave it behind and we are able to live in today.

CHAPTER 10

Self-Acceptance

Self-Parenting Step 10:

Practiced daily self-acceptance and learned to live in the present.

Look to this day,
For it is life,
The very life of life . . .
For yesterday is but a dream,
And tomorrow is only a vision,
But today, well lived,
Makes every yesterday a dream of happiness
And every tomorrow a vision of hope . . .

Sanskrit Proverb

I can't get to sleep. My inner child will not let me go.
. . . Finally I put out my hand, draw her into the bed
and cuddle her, caress her cheek, rub her back, stroke
her hair — and we both slip into slumber.

Excerpt from I.P.'s self-parenting retreat journal

Living In The Present . . .

The gift of living in the present is one of the greatest we can give our inner child. "Living in the now" is a way of being, of exploring and of sending and spending energy that complements the spontaneity of our inner child. In learning how to savor each present moment, we can make a conscious break with the past and give up anxiety about the future.

The starting place, as it was when we were children, is learning about our bodies.

. . . In Our Bodies

Prepare to ask your inner child for assistance.

Let your inner child appear in the form of a beam of light within you. Visualize the beam of light moving about you. As the light touches each part of your body, have your inner child ask that part how it feels, what it needs.

Ask your inner child to help you learn the physical and emotional needs attached to each part of your body. Talk with her as she answers your questions.

How is your head, your scalp, cheeks, eyes, ears, nose, mouth, teeth?

What part of your head needs more attention than it's been getting?

What type of attention does it need?

How is your upper body, your neck, shoulders, back, chest, arms?

What part of your upper body needs more attention?

What type of attention does it need?

How is your stomach — your *hara,* the center of your energy, the place where you were connected to your birth mother?

What type of attention does it need?

Your genitals?

What type of attention do they need?

How is your lower body, your buttocks, thighs, calves, feet?

What part needs more attention?

What type of attention does it need?

Practicing *Do-In*

Make a loose fist and gently and lovingly tap each of the parts of your body you have discussed with your inner child. This is *do-in,* the Japanese art of self-massage. *Do-in* (pronounced "doh-in") is another means of living in the present by learning how your body feels.

Take your time with this. Allow your inner child to join you in the spirit of play. Allow yourself to be noisy, to moan or joyfully shout if the spirit moves you.

Begin with your head. Tap each part beginning with your scalp and work your way down to your eyes. Then tap with fingertips, as you caress your nose, mouth, cheeks, ears and throat.

Notice how you feel — where you find tension, where it feels just great to be touched.

Again make loose fists and tap your chest and your arms. Tap up and down each arm three times. Bend over and gently tap out your back.

Notice how you feel. Note where you hold tension. Note where it feels wonderful to be touched.

Gently tap clockwise around your stomach. Bend over and more vigorously tap out your buttocks.

Notice how you feel. Note if you find tension in any one area. Allow yourself to know where you need to be touched more.

Now vigorously, without hurting yourself, tap up and down your legs three times. Kick off your shoes and slap the soles of your feet.

How do you feel? Are you holding tension in your legs or feet? Where do you need to be touched more?

Now swing your arms from side to side. Jump up and down if you like and shake yourself all over.

Connect to your physical self through *do-in.*

Living Consciously

Many of us lead such rushed lives, it is difficult to stay in contact with our physical selves. Under stress, we may dream of dramatically changing our lives, of moving to a tropical island or a continental city. Such a drastic change is not necessary because nurturance is available to us every day in living consciously through self-parenting.

Practice being conscious of how you feel as you go about your day. Ask your inner child to be by your side as you go through your day.

As you shower or bathe, do so consciously. Ask each part of your body how it feels, what it needs.

For example: How does your scalp feel as you shampoo it? Does it like to be scrubbed hard in some areas, softly in others?

How does your face feel when you wash it, your fingers smoothly gliding through the rich soapy lather? Is your touch loving? How does your inner child feel as you lovingly cleanse your skin?

Do you wash your genitals lovingly? Or do you just rush through your bath? How does it feel to wash this tender part of your body lovingly?

How does it feel to stroke your arms and legs?

How does it feel to wash your feet? Do they crave more attention?

Are there other parts of your body that ask for more attention?

Note where they are and what they need.

As you brush your teeth, do you take the time to clean each tooth or do you rush? Do you take the time to rinse your mouth and to floss? Do you smile at yourself in the mirror and admire your beautiful teeth?

As you pick out your clothes for the day, do you choose what will make you feel your best? How does it feel to make this decision?

Notice how you feel as you get dressed. Try stretching as you place your arms in your sleeves. How does this feel?

As you look in the mirror, smile to yourself instead of looking for imperfections. Notice how this changes your face and be aware of how you feel.

As you walk, lift your shoulders and stand up straighter. Sit straighter, as you did when you were a child. Note how this feels.

As you eat, listen to your body and feed yourself only what your body asks. Try to do this throughout the day. See if you choose water instead of coffee, fruit instead of cookies, nuts instead of chocolate.

When you feel the urge to urinate or to have a bowel movement, take care of these needs instead of putting them off. Let yourself notice how this feels.

As you have physical contacts today — hugging, kissing or just sitting or standing next to someone — notice how you feel.

If you are sexually intimate today, let yourself be aware of how your body feels as you make love. Is this different for you than on other occasions? Note how you feel.

As you fall asleep tonight, make yourself consciously comfortable. Do something special for yourself: fluff your pillows; savor a cup of warm milk; read a favorite poem; meditate on the words of a prayer.

Can you think of a conscious daily practice you would like to add for yourself? Do it!

. . . The Next Day

How many of these conscious daily practices are you comfortable in keeping?

Note which practices you do keep.

Set a goal and make a statement of personal intention for the ones you want to keep.

Wearing Our Lives As Loose Garments

"I have learned silence from the talkative, tolerance from the intolerant and kindness from the unkind. I should not be ungrateful to those teachers," poignantly wrote Kahlil Gibran. And so it has been with us. The Creator has provided each of us with many teachers. Which lessons we remember are a matter of our own choosing.

As we embrace knowledge about ourselves, it is important to know we can wear our lives like loose garments. We do this by keeping daily events in perspective, dealing with what we can at any given moment and, most importantly, leaving the rest for later. We can keep our recovery in perspective by accepting the process and trusting our journey through it. If, for example, we are angry at our parents, we must own this feeling, put our arms around it and, in acceptance, make peace with it.

Wearing our lives like a loose garment can also help us as we take neither ourselves nor others too seriously.

Ethel Barrymore once said, "You grow up the day you have your first real laugh — at yourself." And it can be the same for us.

Remember As Children . . .

We found delight in many moments.

Our bodies were the first worlds we encountered and, as we knew them, we loved them.

We loved how we looked. We smiled at our own reflections.

We found joy in "first times," in the power and mastery of being able to do things for ourselves.

We allowed ourselves to feel and to know our bodies and we loved our bodies.

We were spontaneous in responding to our bodily needs and functions.

We took pleasure in our genital organs.

We ate what was right for us and not more, often much to our parents' concern.

We struggled until we sat, walked, talked. We did this and had great joy in our accomplishments.

We naturally did what would make us feel good about ourselves.

When we were hurt, we would kiss the sore place to help it heal.

Guidelines

Affirm yourself by practicing daily conscious living.

Allow yourself to live in your body and to remain in touch with what your physical self needs.

Allow yourself to remain in touch with your physical self through practicing *do-in* or another form of self-massage.

Allow yourself to live so you are consciously in touch with your needs and wants when you are with your loved ones, your co-workers and your friends.

Allow yourself conscious daily knowledge of your spiritual needs.

CHAPTER 11

Finding The Divinity Within

Self-Parenting Step 11:

Allowed the divinity in us to shine forth by surrendering to our Higher Power.

We are not human beings sharing our spiritual experience. We are spiritual beings sharing our human experience.

Anonymous

Meditate on your Self, worship your Self, kneel to your Self, understand your Self; your God dwells within you as you.

Swami Muktananda

To H.P.

It makes sense to me that there must be spirituality in my direction. What is it though? What would you have me be? I like the idea to do and enjoy and the path will be given to me. I like breaking free of the old traditions, of choosing a religion separate from my spiritual life.

I believe the answers are in solitude, enjoyment and love. I believe that everything can be spiritual. I believe you want me to be all I can be.

Excerpt from R.C.'s letter to his Higher Power

Our Higher Parent And Our Higher Power

When we were lost or scared as children, we naturally turned to that part of us which helped us figure out what to do. When our parents were unable to take care of themselves and we needed, even as little children, to take care of them, there was a part of us that had the answers and helped us accomplish tasks beyond our age. Our Higher Parent was that part of ourselves which guided us.

Each of us has a Higher Parent within us who transcends the circumstances of our lives and helps us find solutions to our problems. Our Higher Parent is the seat of our intuitive knowledge. Our Higher

Parent is the seat of the inner wisdom which flows from the divinity within us. Our Higher Parent is our direct channel to our Higher Power. To the degree to which we learn to gain access to our Higher Parent, we are able to trust in our inner resources and find solutions for our problems. When we turn to our Higher Parent for help, we find the ability to move from the dark times into the light of our own spirituality.

Unlike our Higher Parent, which is within us, our Higher Power is the universal consciousness. Our Higher Power exists in the universe and is the source of life in all things; it is the ultimate reality. Each of us may have a different concept of it but what we call our Higher Power is unimportant. How we incorporate a Higher Power into our lives is what matters. Our Higher Parent helps us incorporate our Higher Power in our lives.

Prepare to learn how to incorporate your Higher Power into your life.

Clear your mind of everyday thoughts.

Imagine a candle burning in front of you.

Focus on the light from that candle.

See your Higher Parent coming toward you.

Ask your Higher Parent to help you find ways to bring your Higher Power into your life.

When your Higher Parent has finished speaking to you, write down what you have experienced.

Maintaining The Daily Presence Of God

Love all God's creation, the whole and every grain of sand. Love every leaf, every ray of God's light. Love the animals, love the plants, love everything. If you love everything, you will perceive the divine mystery in things.

Fyodor Dostoyevsky

As children we were as one with universal consciousness. We naturally loved everything in life. We did not feel any separation between us, our mother earth and our Higher Power. We did not need to learn to communicate with our Higher Power because we were in contact with it all the time.

When we practice the 11th Step, we learn to live with God consciousness. We learn to keep God as a "background thought," maintaining an inner spiritual focus at all times, regardless of what we are doing. We keep a constant consciousness that we are all children of the light. We love all things.

Living As An Act Of Prayer

When we have true spiritual consciousness, we live each day as a prayer. When we live each day as a prayer, we assume the responsibility of making our primary purpose the realization of ourselves as spiritual beings. We seek the divinity in others and we see ourselves and others at all times as spiritual beings.

Let us prepare to experience our inner divinity and learn how to live as an act of prayer.

Imagine you are walking with your inner child.

You are holding his hand.

A bright light surrounds you and your inner child. It is the healing light of the Creator's love.

Invite someone you love into the light.

Feel your love. Feel the healing energy of the light.

Now invite someone you are having trouble with into the light.

Feel your hate and anger melt. Feel your heart open. Feel your forgiveness for this person.

Acknowledge you are both children of the Higher Power.

When the visualization ends, write down your experience.

Meditation: Surrendering To Our Higher Power

Many of us living in Western cultures are confused about meditation. We may not understand how to meditate and are frightened of the concept. Most of us find the process too passive. Spiritual listening skills are underdeveloped in Western society, where technological achievements are more valued than spiritual insight. This onesidedness is one reason why we have accomplished so much as a society but still feel empty on a personal level.

Meditation is the art of developing spiritual listening skills. It is looking within and can be practiced in many ways. It does not have to be complicated. It can be chanting or visualization or simply looking at a flower or just watching the rain. Try this exercise based on one suggested by Swami Muktananda in his book *Meditate*.

Let your breath move naturally and watch it. Do not force anything.

Become immersed in your own inner self. Turn your mind and senses inward.

If thoughts arise let them come and go.

Meditate with the awareness that you are a witness of the mind.

The moment your thoughts become still, the light of your Higher Power will shine through.

When your meditation is complete, write down your experience.

Remember that, like anything else, meditation will yield results only to the degree it is done on a regular basis. As Kahlil Gibran wrote, "When I planted my pain in the field of patience, it bore the fruit of happiness." This is the promise realized through the practice of daily meditation.

Prayer

Prayer is different from meditation. Prayer is asking God for help. It is the raising of our consciousness toward the Higher Power. It is turning over our will and surrendering to our Higher Power.

The Bible promises that when we become as children, the kingdom of heaven will open to us. As children we prayed naturally. Our hearts were open to God and we asked for help and guidance without shame or pride. We did not need to know formal prayers. We made up our own from our hearts, with sincerity and love.

As we grew older, we lost our spiritual innocence and no longer prayed spontaneously. Many of us became stuck in the rigidity of formal prayer. We forgot how to pray from our hearts.

Let us prepare to pray again from our hearts.

Let us prepare to pray as children again.

Breathe deeply and let yourself relax. Focus your eyes on a nearby object and let your consciousness drift.

See your inner child coming toward you.

Ask your inner child to help you open a channel to your Higher Power.

Ask your inner child to help you write a prayer from his heart to your Higher Power.

Let the prayer come naturally from your inner child.

When it is written, read the prayer and recite it from your heart.

Let your Higher Parent tell you how she feels about your prayer.

Write down your experience.

Allowing The Divinity Within

As Swami Muktananda wrote in *In The Company Of A Siddha,* "If you want to see God, you don't have to pursue God or follow any religion. Just shower your compassion on people without any expectation, and then God will reveal Himself to you."

This is the secret of becoming connected with our inner divinity. In the supreme awareness that we are all one, we become free. When we can look on the inhabitants of the rest of the world as our brothers and sisters and mean it, when we can move to that moment of divine consciousness when we see no difference between us and anyone else including our enemies, then we allow the divinity within us to shine through.

We existed in this state of unconditional love as children. We return to this state when we sincerely practice Step 11.

Remember As Children . . .

We were conscious of being one with God.

We did not have to learn to communicate with our Higher Power because we were in contact with our Higher Power all the time.

We turned naturally to our Higher Parent for help.

We did not see ourselves as separate from other people.

We naturally loved every living thing.

We took joy in nature. We were able to spontaneously appreciate the world around us.

We loved ourselves and others unconditionally.

We prayed naturally from our hearts.

Guidelines

Practice the presence of God in your life by keeping God as a background thought.

Commit yourself to the awareness that all people are the same, as children of God.

Commit yourself to meditate daily.

Affirm your Higher Parent and your ability to gain access to great inner resources.

Commit yourself to loving each living thing as you would your own child.

Live each day as an act of prayer.

Allow yourself to feel your compassion for other people.

Allow yourself to feel love and forgiveness for those who hurt you.

Commit yourself to honoring the divinity within by keeping an inner focus at all times.

CHAPTER 12

Giving Back Your Best — Creating A New Tomorrow

Self-Parenting Step 12:

Having had this spiritual awakening, we reached out to others in the spirit of giving, love and community.

I believe that man will not merely endure. He will prevail. He is immortal, not because he alone among creatures has an inexhaustible voice, but because he has a soul, a spirit capable of compassion and sacrifice and endurance.

William Faulkner, on accepting the Nobel Prize

Dear sunshine and nature and warmth and gardens and smells and air and apples on trees and snow and fields,
I can feel life's vibrations when I can feel my own feelings and my own needs and this releases my love, my energy. God will shine through me. I can take my hands and pull back the thick dark big black curtains on each side and though they are heavy, I can lift them back and in the slit between them, see the warm, pink light, see my self, know my self, feel my truth, know my truth, my needs, my joys, my pains and express them, if only in the serenity of being there. I am connected — this outside with this inside.

Excerpt from N.N.'s letter to her Higher Parent

You Cannot Keep It Unless You Give It Away

There is a saying in Alcoholics Anonymous that "You can't keep it unless you give it away." This means that any individual's sobriety continues only if its benefits are shared with alcoholics who are still suffering. The saying holds true also for adult children from dysfunctional families. We will not be able to maintain our own growth unless we find ways to give back to our families, friends and community the benefits of our recovery.

This giving back is called service. It is the cornerstone of recovery. It is the basis for continuing spiritual growth. Building service into our lives is important because we cannot truly be considered recovering if we do not give back to the world the gifts we have received.

As children we gave naturally to others without expecting anything in return. We were part of the human family without reservation. Unconditional love was our basic state. But as we grew up and were faced with conditional love from our parents, we lost our sense of generosity and began to withhold our love from the world.

As adults many of us have misconceptions based upon our religious beliefs about service. Some of us perform charitable acts out of a sense of duty and obligation. We expect credit for being "good." This is not service.

Service is done with joy. It does not look for recognition. It does not come from the ego, the doing is enough. Service is extending a hand, feeding the hungry, housing the homeless, caring for an addicted infant, sponsoring someone in a 12-Step program. Service is sharing our stories of sickness and recovery with someone still in pain and darkness. It's helping a child still living in an alcoholic or drug-addicted family. For many of us, service means just being good parents.

Service Inventory

Let us make an inventory of how we are giving back our gifts.

Invite your Higher Parent to help you.

See him clearly before you.

Ask him to help you make an honest list of how you give back:

To your family:

To your community:

To your 12-Step program:

To your Higher Power:

Examine the inventory.

Where do you need to do more?

Write a plan showing how you will improve your service inventory.

Remember that giving service creates depth in us. It opens our hearts to the world. Unexpressed love withers. Service to others is the highest expression of our Creator's love to us.

Feeling Our Resistance — Parenting Our Inner Child

Many of us probably felt resistance as we did the preceding exercise. Our inner child often rebels against the discipline and selflessness it takes to give service. When we self-parent, we learn to handle resistance as it arises. We do not give over to resistance as we did before we became healthy and responsible for our lives.

It is necessary to bring to the surface the resistance our inner child feels about doing service or she will undermine our ability to follow through on the 12th Step. Our inner child fears that there will not be enough time for her if anything or anyone else gets our attention. She needs to be reassured.

Prepare to have a dialogue with your inner child.

Clear your mind. Focus on a nearby object.

See your inner child standing before you.

Let her tell you how she feels about your giving time to service.

Write down what she says to you, using the hand opposite to your dominant hand.

Now respond to your inner child. Assure her there will be time for her.

Hold her close. Let her know you will always be available to her.

Becoming A Drum Major

Martin Luther King, Jr., said, ". . . If you want to say that I was a drum major, say that I was a drum major for justice; say that I was a drum major for peace; say I was a drum major for righteousness. And all of the other shallow things will not matter."

Dr. King understood what really counted in life. In his speech, he stated that he did not have money to leave behind for his children and he wasn't able to leave luxurious material possessions to his family.

In fact, his legacy was much greater because it was the example of a committed life.

Each of us needs to decide what kind of drum major we will be. We need to consider whether we will lead committed lives, lives that show a purpose greater than ourselves.

Let us prepare to find the higher purpose in our lives.

Relax and breathe deeply. Close your eyes.

See your Higher Parent coming toward you.

Feel the serenity emanating from this source of inner wisdom.

Ask your Higher Parent to help you gain insight into a higher purpose for yourself.

Let yourself be open to the answer.

Write down what your Higher Parent says.

Remember the words of John F. Kennedy, "The credit belongs to the man who is actually in the arena, whose face is marred by dust and sweat and blood, who knows the great enthusiasms, the great devotions and spends himself in a worthy cause." Each of us needs, as part of our recovery and growth, to find that worthy cause.

Being A Role Model — Teaching Others

"There is only one way in which one can endure man's inhumanity to man, and that is to try, in one's own life, to exemplify man's humanity to man." This is how Alan Paton, author of *Cry the Beloved Country,* summarizes what each individual must do to face and overcome the horror in the world.

There is much inhumanity in the world. Many of us experienced it as children. Now many of us have been caught in the trap of repeating the behaviors we hated as children. We have ended up abusing our children or spouses the way we were abused. In this way we continue the legacy of inhumanity in the world.

As we work to show the example of man's humanity to man, we break the cycle of pain into which we were born. We become changed role models for our children and all people around us. We bring light into the world. We become candles lighting the darkness.

Let us prepare to look at what kind of role models we are.

Take a deep breath and focus on a nearby object.

See your Higher Parent coming toward you.

Ask your Higher Parent to help you.

List in what ways you are a role model as:

A spouse or lover:

A friend:

A parent:

An employee:

A community member:

A spiritual person:

A 12-Step program member:

Review the list to see where you need to make more of an effort.

Now make a commitment to make some improvement as a role model each day and to tell no one about what you have done. Let your focus be on small things, acts or tasks that you can accomplish in the course of a day.

As Helen Keller said, "I long to accomplish a great and noble task but it is my chief duty to accomplish small tasks as if they were great and noble." Remember it is the small things which lead to great character.

Co-dependent No More

As children we saw God in all things. We believed in ourselves and others. We had dreams for ourselves and we believed in those dreams.

As we grew older, we became co-dependent and we began to believe that we could rely only on ourselves. We became entangled in a web of compulsive self-reliance. We lost our faith in a Higher Power and we lost touch with our own spirituality.

In recovery from the effects of our dysfunctional childhoods, we come back to that state of spiritual innocence where we began. As we grow in spirituality, we leave our co-dependency behind.

When we become healthy:

- We have changed our responses.
- We see options.
- We make choices.
- We are motivated from within, not without.
- We no longer need to relive trauma in order to feel.
- We learn to move on with our lives.

Now take another look at the list you have just read. How does it help you measure how you are progressing in leaving co-dependency behind?

Ask your Higher Parent to help you assess how you are doing in each of these areas.

Talk with your Higher Parent about areas where you have grown and ask his guidance in seeing where you still need to grow.

Use this as a blueprint for continued growth.

Sharing The Light

We are the winners . . . the survivors . . . the ones who endured through the dark nights of childhood to become loving, whole people. We are the promise of recovery realized. The light that shines in us is a light in the darkness for those still lost in co-dependency and addiction. We are the future. We can create new beginnings for ourselves, our families and our communities.

As Dr. Martin Luther King, Jr., said, "Unarmed truth and unconditional love will have the final word in reality. This is why right, temporarily defeated, is stronger than evil triumphant."

In facing the world with unarmed truth and unconditional love, we cannot fail in our recovery. We will, as Dr. King told us, "Be there in love and justice and in truth and commitment to others, so that we can make of this old world a new world."

Remember As Children . . .

We gave to one another naturally without need to receive something in exchange.

We saw God in everything.

We gave our best at all times without resentment.

We believed in ourselves and others.

We looked for the goodness in other people.

We believed in our dreams for the future.

Guidelines

Practice doing service for your fellow passengers on Spaceship Earth.

Find a purpose bigger than yourself.

Do one kind thing a day for someone else and don't tell anyone about it.

Treat with respect everything you do, even the smallest task.

Affirm your basic nature as a loving spiritual person.

Affirm the truth that we are all children of God.

Believe in yourself and see the best in others.

Acknowledge your role as a member of the human family.

THE 12 STEPS TO SELF-PARENTING

1. Admitted our powerlessness to change our past — that our lives had become unmanageable and became willing to surrender to our love and not to our fear.

2. Found hope in the belief that recovery is possible through faith and an acceptance of the fact that we are never really alone.

3. Learned to let go of compulsive self-reliance by reaching out to our Higher Parent.

4. Made an honest assessment of our strengths and weaknesses and accepted the impact our childhood has had on us as adults.

5. Learned to share our self-parenting issues with others without self-recrimination or shame.

6. Became ready to change by giving up the demand to be perfect.

7. Learned to embrace our uniqueness and connectedness to others in a spirit of love and humility.

8. Learned self-forgiveness and made amends to our inner child.

9. Healed our inner child by realizing the promises of self-parenting in our daily living.

10. Practiced daily self-acceptance and learned to live in the present.

11. Allowed the divinity in us to shine forth by surrendering to our Higher Power.

12. Having had this spiritual awakening, we reached out to others in the spirit of giving, love and community.

BIBLIOGRAPHY

Bradshaw, John. **Bradshaw On: The Family.** Pompano Beach, FL: Health Communications, 1988.

Capacchione, Lucia. **The Power Of Your Other Hand: A Course In Channelling The Inner Wisdom Of The Right Brain.** N. Hollywood, CA: Newcastle Publishing, 1988.

Fosdick, Harry Emerson. **Riverside Preachers: Fosdick/McCracken/Campbell/Coffin.** New York: Pilgrim Press, 1978.

Fossom, Merle A. and Mason, Marilyn J. **Facing Shame: Families in Recovery.** New York: Norton, 1986.

Frankl, Viktor E. **The Doctor Of The Soul.** New York: Knopf, 1965.

Gibran, Kahlil. **The Prophet.** New York: Knopf, 1958.

Livingstone, Jeanne. **Brother Lion.** Deerfield Beach, FL: Health Communications, 1988.

Muktananda, Swami. **Meditate.** Albany, NY: State U. NY Press, 1980.

_____ **In The Company Of A Siddha.** South Fallsberg, NY: SYDA Found., 1981.

Oliver-Diaz, Philip and O'Gorman, Patricia A. **12 Steps To Self-Parenting.** Deerfield Beach, FL: Health Communications, 1988.

_____ **Breaking The Cycle Of Addiction.** Pompano Beach, FL: Health Communications, 1987.

Paton, Alan. **Cry The Beloved Country.** New York: MacMillan, 1948, 1986.

The Twelve Steps For Christians. Deerfield Beach, FL: Health Communications, 1989.

The Twelve Steps — A Spiritual Journey. Deerfield Beach, FL: Health Communications, 1988.

Books from . . .
Health Communications